THE
RAPTORS
ALL F-15 AND F-16 AERIAL COMBAT VICTORIES
DONALD J. McCARTHY JR.

EG
58 FS
AF790078

CONTENTS

DEDICATED TO THE MEMORY

It would have been impossible to complete this project without the help and support of my family and friends, who have always given their time and above all their encouragement. I wish to offer my thanks and sincere appreciation to those who have always given of themselves to help me, and I dedicate this book to their memory. Chief boatswains mate (MDV) Donald J. McCarthy, USN (Ret.), WWII—Korean War; AIC Donald J. McCarthy III; James L. Nichols, USAF; A2C James W. Finnegan, USAF, Korean War; A2C John J. Macione, USAF—Korean War; Sgt. William Clark, USA—WWII; A2C Thomas W. Viens, USAF; 1st Sgt. James A. Perkins, USA, WWII; William E. McGuire, USA, Korean War; Capt. Gene Eskew, USAF—Vietnam; Lt. Joseph A. San Juan, Connecticut Army National Guard, (Ret.); Tech. Sgt. Harvey O. Thorp, late Connecticut ANG; Sgt. Michael I. Cope, USMC—Vietnam; Sgt. Joseph "Jeff" Watterson, USMC; Maj. C. Robert Satti, USMC; Seaman Wayne Pelka, USN; Gunnery Sgt. William Smith, USMC—WWII, Korean War; Sgt. Donald Beckum, USA—Vietnam; Lance Cpl. Steve Hancock, USMC—Vietnam; Lance Cpl. Joseph Burgess, USMC—Vietnam; SPC 4 Louis Birchall, USA—Vietnam; Master Sgt. William "Bill" Acky, USAF, (Ret.); Master Sgt. Robert F. Kenary, USAF, (Ret.); Staff Sgt. Harold Monty, USAF; and A1C Mike Manganello, USAF.

ACKNOWLEDGMENTS

I wish to offer a special thanks to the following friends who have opened their photo collections to me; without them this project would never have been completed: Tyler P. Petrini; Maj. Gen. Spence M. "Sam" Armstrong, USAF (Ret.); Cmdr. Peter Mersky, USN (Ret.); Ofer Zidon, Israel; Tsahi and Hagit Ben-Ami, Israel; Amos Dorr, Israel; Azar Zohar, Israel; Elda Eckstein, Israel; Sariel Stiller, Israel; Pat Martin, Canada; Mike Durning; Martin Eadie; Gary Stedman; Martin Timmers; Mithat Ozdogan; William Shenley; Kevin Daws; Bruce Smith; Robert Kolek; Senior Airman Taylor Curry; David F. Brown; Titan Miller; Gerard Helmer; Najam Khan, Pakistan; Sayed Zohalb; Jonathan Derden; A1C John Linzmeier; Sgt. Kevin Foy; Jeff Puzzullo; Maj. David Erff, USAF (Ret.); Chris Pelka; Sgt. Roger Reed, Waterford, Connecticut, Police Department; Inspector Michael Hurley, state's attorney office; and Mithat Ozdogan. Others to whom I am truly indebted for their encouragement with this project: Leah N. Petrini, Nicolas I. Petrini, Natalie R. Petrini, and Kaylee, Mac, and Zac Deer.

INTRODUCTION

The Korean War (25 June 1950–27 July 1953) was the first post-WWII experience that pitted American and United Nation (UN) forces in the first jet aerial combat in the skies over North Korea. The American F-86 Sabers dueled with Mikoyan-Gurevich MiG-15 Fagots in fast jet air combat. The combat record of the F-86 against North Korean MiG-15s was most impressive. The first confirmed MiG kill was claimed by Lt. Col. Bruce H. Hinton, USAF. United States Air Force pilots would claim over 792 aerial victories as a result of aerial combat against the MiG with the loss of only 78 Sabers; postwar research indicates a more realistic figure of 397 to 500 USAF victories. Jet vs. jet aerial warfare came of age during the Korean War.

After 3 years, 1 month, and 2 days of aerial warfare, what lessons did military and political leadership take from the Korean War? The combined genius of military and political leadership falsely believed the day of jet vs. jet air combat was history. They had convinced themselves that all future air engagements would involve beyond visual range (BVR) air battles. The concept of beyond visual range air combat led to the development and deployment for the United States Navy and Air Force the F-4 Phantom II. The ill-conceived belief was the Phantom II, with its air-to-air missiles, would have the ability to engage massive antagonistic government bomber formations (Russian – Chinese) at long range.

Many other lessons were learned during the Korean War, but they would go unheeded, only to resurface twelve years later in the skies over North Vietnam.

During the war in Southeast Asia (1965–1973), United States Air Force, Navy, and Marine pilots flew approximately 5.25 million sorties over South Vietnam, North Vietnam, Northern and Southern Laos, and Cambodia. The combined air forces of the United States and its allies dropped 6,727,084 tons of bombs in Indo China, compared with 2,700,000 tons dropped on Germany during WWII.

In the eight years the United States was involved in Southeast Asia, it lost almost 10,000 fixed wing aircraft and helicopters to North Vietnamese antiaircraft artillery (AAA), surface-to-air missiles (SAMs), and North Vietnamese MiGs.

The loss of 10,000 aircraft is insignificant when we compare the numbers of Americans killed in action (58,303) or wounded (153,303).

There is no doubt the Vietnam War ended in frustration for many of us that served in Southeast Asia during the war years. Fortunately, many of the Air Force and Navy combat pilots of the Vietnam era would remain in uniform and eventually become senior military leaders; they either publicly or privately vowed the mistakes of the Vietnam War would not be repeated.

Mr. Drew Middleton stated in his introduction to the book *Air War-Vietnam*, produced by the United States Air Force, 1978; "Vietnam was the first war fought with the new weapons. No war in the future will be unaffected by its technological and tactical weapons."

Mr. Middleton's assertion proved to be quite profound, as a new generation of aerial combat tactics and technological advances in aircraft design would revolutionize how the United States would continue to control battle space in aerial combat. The United States would produce two world-class multi-role fourth generation tactical fighters in the McDonnell Douglas (now Boeing) F-15 Eagle and the General Dynamics (now Lockheed Martin) F-16 Falcon.

The F-15 Eagle was created with the philosophy "not a pound for air-to-ground." The Eagle had one mission when the jet became operational: to be an all-weather fighter capable of gaining and maintaining air superiority in aerial combat.

For nearly forty years, the F-15 Eagle has served with the United States Air Force and several foreign air forces. The Eagle has performed in combat far above the expectations of the original designers of the aircraft. The F-15 was first taken into combat by the Israeli Air and Space Force (IASF) on 27 June 1979, when Capt. Moshe Melnik, flying in F-15 Baz ("Eagle") 663, shot down a Syrian MiG-21 with a Python 3 air-to-air-missile. Between 7–11 June 1982, the "Double Tail" Squadron of the IASF claimed 33 enemy aircraft destroyed; as of today, along with the "Spearhead" Squadron, they have been credited with 53 kills without a single loss.

In this book you will find not one or two photographs of the Israeli F-15 Bazs credited with a MiG kill while deployed in front line service, but *all* of them. With each MiG killer photograph you will also learn the identity of the pilot, squadron, tail number, and kill weapons deployed in the destruction of the enemy aircraft. Lastly, the reader will find the Hebrew nicknames of all of the F-15s with their English translation (i.e., F-15 Baz No. 663, nickname Hamadlik / Fire Igniter).

The United States Air Force would not claim their first aerial victory in the Eagle until the Gulf War on 17 January 1991, when Capt. Jon K. "JB" Kelk, flying F-15 Eagle tail number 85-0125, destroyed an Iraqi MiG-29 with an AIM-7M radar missile. USAF F-15 Eagles would claim a total of 34 Iraqi aircraft in aerial combat during the Gulf War. The United States Air Force would also claim an additional 4 MiG-29 kills during Operation ALLIED FORCE. Like the Israeli Air and Space Force, the United States Air Force, with its 38 F-15 Eagle victories, has yet to lose a single Eagle in air-to-air combat. Like the IASF, there are not just a few photographs of the USAF F-15 MiG killers, but every Eagle credited with a MiG, Mirage, or Sukhoi aerial victory.

There is no doubt the F-15 Eagles of the American-led coalition were the dominant fighter aircraft during Operation DESERT STORM, but there were a small number of other aircraft credited with aerial combat victories. In chapter 8, the reader will be introduced to a number of aircraft that made aviation history, namely the United States Navy F/A-18 Hornets that claimed their first ever aerial victories, and the United States Air Force's two Warthogs that claimed the first ever kills for the A-10A Thunderbolts.

The Israelis were first to see the true potential of their F-15 fleet on 1 October 1985, when they surprised the world with the successful execution of Operation MIVTZA REGELETZ ("WOODEN LEG"), a retaliatory raid against the PLO headquarters in Hammam al-Shatt, Tunisia. Even today many aspects of the Tunisia raid are still classified. In researching the mission, the F-15 strike aircraft involved in the raid have been identified and photographs of the F-15 Bazs that participated in the raid are included.

Often overlooked is the F-15 aerial victory of Capt. Ayhed Salah Al-Shamrani of the Royal Saudi Air Force, who on 24 January 1991 engaged and destroyed two Iraqi Mirage F-1EQs that were targeting coalition military vessels operating in the Gulf. During the engagement the Saudi captain was flying F-15 No. 509. At some time after the war No. 509's tail number was changed to No. 1308.

Joining the US Air Force and Israeli Air and Space Force F-15s in dominating the battle space in the skies and on the ground is the General Dynamics (now Lockheed Martin) F-16 multi-role fighter. The F-16 has continued to successfully evolve into an all-weather dog fighter and strike aircraft.

Today, the American designed and built F-16 Falcon is deployed with many (25) allied nations throughout the world. Like the F-15 Eagle, the F-16 first saw combat with the Israelis, who renamed the F-16 Netz ("Sparrowhawk"). Ever since its introduction on 17 August 1978, the F-16 has proven itself an agile and outstanding dog fighter. Besides the IASF, the USAF, Pakistani Air Force, Royal Netherlands Air Force, Venezuelan Air Force, and most recently the Turkish Air Force have all claimed aerial victories in the F-16.

Photographs of all of the Israeli and American F-16s with confirmed aerial combat victories to date are included. Also presented are photographs of F-16 Netz No. 107, the world's all time leading MiG killer with 6.5 kills. The iconic F-16 Netz No. 107 also has the distinction of flying in Operation OPERA as Eshkol 02.

You will also discover photographs of F-16 Falcon tail no. 89-2009, flown by Capt. Robert G. White (USAF), who in a single sortie shot down 3 Serbian Air Force Soko J-21 Jastrebs.

The Afghanistan Civil War saw the Pakistani Air Force drawn into conflict with Afghanistani and Russian aircraft. From 1986–1988, the Pakistani Air Force confirms their F-16s destroyed 10 Afghan and Russian aircraft that intruded into Pakistani airspace. Flight Lt. Khalid Mahmood has been identified by the PAF as having four aerial victories in three different F-16s (Nos. 85728, 84717, and 85711) between 12 September 1988 and 31 January 1989. Rounding out the known aerial victories for the F-16 are confirmed kills by the Royal Netherlands Air Force (MiG-29) and the Turkish Air Force (one MiG-23 and two Mi-8 helicopters).

In chapter 10, photographs of all eight F-16 Netz of Eshkol and Izmal flights that participated in Operation OPERA on 7 June 1981 are displayed, along with information identifying the pilots, call signs, and weapons deployed during the mission.

In chapter 1, the reader will discover outstanding photographs of the all-time leading United States Air Force F-4D Phantom II MiG killer (tail number 66-7436), credited with 6 confirmed kills during the Vietnam War, along with a Vietnam-era color photograph of the leading Republic F-105 Thunderchief MiG killer (tail number 62-4282, with 3 confirmed kills). Chapter 3 includes the all-time leading Israeli F-4E Phantom II MiG killer Kurnass ("Sledgehammer") No. 109, with 7 aerial victories. Kurnass No. 109 was lost in a mid-air collision with an Israeli A-4 Ahit ("Eagle").

The majority of the photographs are in color and clearly depict the unique aircraft markings of national air forces operating Eagles and Falcons, with particular interest in the new tail art that has been applied to the F-15 Bazs and F-16 Netz of the Israeli Air and Space Force.

Every attempt has been made to obtain and use only the highest quality photographs. A number of photographs were found not suitable for publication, but are of great significance in the aerial combat history of the F-15 Eagle and F-16 Falcon. With the help of Najam Khan of Pakistan, four of these aircraft have been computer generated and the finished digital artwork has been included.

CHAPTER 1

EVOLUTION OF THE McDONNELL DOUGLAS F-15 EAGLE AND GENERAL DYNAMICS F-16 FALCON

The McDonnell Douglas F-15 Eagle and General Dynamics F-16 Fighting Falcon ultimately derived from the Vietnam War. The air war in Southeast Asia (SEA) bravely carried out by American Air Force and Navy pilots proved the United States was truly in need of a new generation of aircraft and weapons.

The United States deployed a bewildering variety of aircraft that saw action in Vietnam, among them the McDonnell Douglas F-4 Phantom II, Republic F-105 Thunderchief, and the Vought F-8 Crusader. The Phantom II, Thunderchief, and Crusader have all secured their place in the combat history of the Vietnam War. The contributions of these aircraft and the sacrifices of their aircrews did more to enhance the evolution process that brought forth the F-15 and F-16 Raptors.

The dictionary defines evolution as "a gradual process in which something changes into a different and usually more complex or better form." The F-4 Phantom II and F-105s of the '60s displayed incredible utility and value as remarkable weapon systems, but the evolutionary process of these aviation icons evolved into a more complex and better form. During their combat service with the United States Air Force and the Zroa Ha' Avir Ve' Halalal (Israeli Air and Space Force), the F-15 Eagle and F-16 Falcon proved to be the world's most prolific fighters, with over 100 aerial combat victories without a single loss. The F-15 Eagle has also been credited with 3 aerial victories with the Royal Saudi Air Force. Since its combat debut with the Israeli Air and Space Force, the General Dynamics F-16 Falcon has claimed well over 59 aerial victories, with the air forces of the United States, Pakistan, and Turkey, also claiming victories with the multi-role fighter.

Southeast Asia

During the air war in Southeast Asia (1965–1973), USAF and USN aircraft, despite being repeatedly challenged by MiGs in the skies over North Vietnam, were credited with only destroying 202 North Vietnamese aircraft in aerial combat. The numbers of aerial victories during the Vietnam War were not anywhere close to the numbers obtained during WWII and Korea. Why?

There have been many theories put forth in books, articles, and even verbal opinions expressed by politicians and military leaders as to why our air-to-air victories during the Vietnam air war did not approach the high numbers of the Korean War.

After the Korean War, our military leadership convinced itself the next major confrontation for the United States would pit our military aircraft against large Russian bomber formations. In the '50s, the USAF, particularly Tactical Air Command (TAC), was oriented more toward nuclear strike missions. If history has taught us anything, it is even the best laid plans of mice and men have a tendency at times to fall apart. Contrary to the brain trust in the Department of Defense, what took place in Southeast Asia was far from air battles against large Russian bomber formations. In reality, what presented itself to the number one military in the world were not large Russian bombers, but a fifth-rate jungle air force with unsophisticated and outdated MiG-17s, MiG-19s, and MiG-21s in comparison to the McDonnell Douglas F-4 Phantom II and Republic F-105 Thunderchief.

One of the most significant and often overlooked reasons for the low air-to-air combat victories during the Vietnam War was the relationship between our senior military and civilian political leadership during the Vietnam era. It is felt by many that high ranking Air Force officers truly did not understand the proper use of tactical air power during the Vietnam War. And just as amazing, and probably more significant, we simply were not prepared to fight the air-to-air war that developed in North Vietnam's skies. As for civilian leadership,

Capts. Richard S. Ritchie and Charles B. DeBellevue shortly after Capt. Ritchie downed his fifth MiG on 28 August 1972 and became the first Air Force ace of the Vietnam War. On 9 September 1972, Capts. DeBellevue and John A. Madden Jr. downed two MiG-19s. Capt. DeBellevue ended the war with six kills, making him the leading Air Force ace of the war. *USAF*

they just simply did not have a clue. Their collective decision making and constant interference clearly demonstrated this.

At the very onset of the Vietnam War, American fighter pilots lacked sufficient training in air combat maneuvering (ACM). An outstanding example of how unprepared United States Air Force pilots were was best set forth by Capt. Steve Ritchie. In a postwar interview Capt. Ritchie addressed the issue of air combat maneuvering. The captain reported on a number of occasions, contrary to the rules of engagement, that some aircrews engaged in mock air-to-air combat, attempting to sharpen their air combat maneuvering skills. This practice obviously worked for Capt. Ritchie, for on 28 August 1972, he became the first and only United States Air Force pilot ace with 5 kills. Capt. Ritchie would be followed in short order by Capt. Charles B. De Bellevue, the highest scoring (6 kills) Air Force ace, and Capt. Jeffery Feinstein (5 kills). Capts. De Bellevue and Feinstein were weapons system officers (WSO), backseaters in the Phantom II.

The first documented ace of the Vietnam air war was not an Air Force pilot, but United States Navy aircrew Lt. Randall H. Cunningham and Lt. (j.g.) William P. Driscoll flying Showtime 100, VF-96, USS *Constellation* (CVA-64).

Coupled with poor air combat maneuvering training, it is a well known fact most combat aircrews heading to Southeast Asia (SEA) never engaged in live fire training with the AIM-7 Sparrow air-to-air missile (semi-active radar type), AIM-9 Sidewinder air-to-air missile (passive IR type), or AIM-4D Falcon air-to-air missile (passive IR type) until deploying. The unreliability and performance limitations of early Sparrow and Sidewinder (45% of AIM-7 and 65% of the AIM-9 failed) air-to-air missiles exacerbated the shortcomings of many air combat crews.

With all the shortfalls with American airframes sent to Southeast Asia (SEA), the four main fighters, along with the three main air-to-air missiles deployed, were responsible for the majority of the MiGs destroyed by American pilots in air-to-air combat.

USAF's leading MiG killer of the Vietnam War with six confirmed aerial victories is "Phantom" F-4D-29-MC-66-7463. The six victories were obtained by five different aircrews during 1972. Today this iconic Phantom is on display at the Air Force Academy, Colorado Springs, Colorado. *D. Jay Collection*

McDonnell Douglas F-4 Phantom II / Republic F-105 Thunderchief

Vought F-8 Crusader

The McDonnell Douglas F-4 Phantom II—a supersonic, all-weather, tandem two-seat, two-engine fighter with beyond visual range (BVR) capabilities—entered service with the Navy in 1960, followed in the mid-'60s by the Marine Corps and Air Force. The multi-task Phantom II was capable of carrying out air superiority, close air support, interception, air defense suppression, long-range strike, fleet defense, and attack and reconnaissance missions.

"Double Ugly" was no down-in-the-dirt dogfighter; when challenged by North Vietnamese MiGs, the Phantom II, in the hands of a skilled pilot and utilizing the Phantom's greatest advantage—its thrust—permitted pilots to engage and disengage in aerial combat at will. This coupling of thrust and skill brought a savage and quick death to North Vietnamese pilots that dared to take on the Phantom II.

USN Phantom pilots claimed 42 aerial combat victories against North Vietnamese MiG-17s and MiG-21s. On 6 June 1965, Commander Louis Page and Lt. John C. Smith Jr. claimed the first American air-to-air victory of the war; the Navy pilots' call sign Sundown 101 destroyed a MiG-17 with an AIM-7D Sparrow air-to-air missile.

The Air Force claimed 137 aerial combat victories over MiGs of the North Vietnamese's Air Force, of which 107½ were credited to the Phantom II. The first USAF MiG kill was claimed by Capts. Thomas S. Roberts and Arthur C. Clark, 45th Tactical Fighter Squadron, 15th Tactical Wing on 10 July 1965. The Air Force pilots (call sign Mink 04) engaged and destroyed a MiG-17 with an AIM-9B Sidewinder air-to-air missile.

F-105 Thunderchief / F-8 Crusader

The Republic F-105 Thunderchief was affectionately known by the ground crews and pilots that took it to war by the nickname "Thud." Whatever name you choose to call this iconic airframe, the Thud was one bad-ass machine. Like the Phantom II, the Thud was never designed with dogfighting in mind.

During the Vietnam War years, the F-105 was the largest single-seat, single engine combat aircraft in history. The Mach 2 capable 105 was originally designed to carry and deliver a single nuclear weapon at high speed.

In the early years of the Vietnam War, the F-105 was without a doubt the dominant strike aircraft conducting missions over North Vietnam. Air Force records indicate the Thunderchief flew over 20,000 sorties; not counting non-combat losses, 382 Thuds were lost in combat. Although less agile than the much smaller MiGs, the 105 shot down 27½ of them. All of the Thud's MiG kills were against North Vietnam's MiG-17: 24½ were shot down by 20 mm cannon fire from the Thud's internal cannon, while 3 kills came by way of its AIM-9 Sidewinder.

The tail code RM in this Vietnam-era photo of 62-4282 indicates the MiG killer was assigned to the 354th TFS, Takhil, RTAFB. The six 750 lb. bombs mounted on the centerline multiple ejection rack clearly indicate the Thud is heading north on another mission "Downtown." The red stars painted on the fuselage below the cockpit denote MiG kills credited to 62-4284. The first two kills were obtained on 10 March 1967 by Capt. Max C. Brestel and the third was credited to Capt. Gene I. Basel. *D. Jay Collection*

The carrier-based Navy Vought F-8 Crusader accounted for 20 aerial combat victories over enemy MiGs. The Crusader is a single-seat, single engine supersonic air superiority jet aircraft. During the Vietnam era the F-8 was also known by a number of nicknames, with "MiG Master" and "Last of the Gunfighters" leading the list.

As a result of the conflict that erupted in the skies over North Vietnam, the Crusader truly earned the moniker "MiG Master"; in head-to-head engagements against Vietnamese MiGs it would claim 20 aerial victories to the loss of only 3 Crusaders. Only four Crusader kills were by 20 mm cannon fire; the remaining kills were accomplished with the AIM-9 Sidewinder. The Crusader would end the war with the best kill ratio of any American fighter.

Post-Vietnam

On 23 January 1973, the nine point Paris Peace Accord was signed and went into effect on 28 January 1973. Not long after the ink had dried, American military leadership reflected on the lessons learned from the Vietnam War. There is no doubt the Phantom II and Thunderchief were the greatest fighter platforms of the Vietnam era, but the United States Air Force and Navy had set a priority! The design of the next generation of fighters would have one purpose: maintaining total air superiority in aerial combat.

The Vietnam War was a rude awakening for United States military. The Air Force's Tactical Air Command (TAC), which bore the brunt of the air war in Vietnam, entered a lengthy period of testing and evaluation. It incorporated the experience of air combat during the war that provided the USAF with justification for the design and manufacture of a truly dedicated air superiority fighter.

The urgency for a new superiority fighter for the Air Force was truly pressed home when the Soviet Union revealed the Mikoyan-Gurevich supersonic interceptor MiG-25 Foxbat in 1967. When the Foxbat entered service in 1970, it had a reported top speed of Mach 2.83 to 3.2, making it one of the fastest aircraft in the world. The MiG-25 featured powerful radar and could carry 4 AA-6 Acrid air-to-air missiles, or a mixture of 2 AA-7 Apex and 2 AA-8 Aphid air-to-air missiles on external pylons.

The search for the Air Force's new fourth generation fighter began in earnest with four aircraft design and manufacturing companies' submitted proposals: General Dynamics was eliminated by the Air Force, while contracts were awarded to Fairchild Republic, North American Rockwell, and McDonnell Douglas. The winning design was announced on 23 December 1969, with the contract going to McDonnell Douglas.

CHAPTER 2
THE RAPTOR COMETH

Raptor is derived from the Latin word *rapere*, meaning to seize or take by force. Raptors are blessed with excellent vision, giving them outstanding ability to detect prey during flight, and have talons and strong beaks that enable them to kill with terrifying precision.

The McDonnell Douglas (now Boeing) F-15 Eagle

The Air Force selected the Eagle design proposal in 1967. The twin engine, all-weather air superiority fighter was originally designed as a single seat tactical fighter. The F-15 was the first dedicated USAF air superiority fighter since the North American F-86 Saber of the Korean War era. Many improvements were made to the Eagle over the Vietnam era Phantom II. The Eagle was built specifically to challenge enemy aircraft over the battlefield with within visual range (WVR) and beyond visual range (BVR) capabilities, and an array of more effective air-to-air missiles. Unlike the early Phantom II, the Eagle featured the standard GAU-4 M61 Vulcan 20 mm, 6-barrel, air cooled rotary cannon, which can typically fire 6,000 rounds a minute.

An F-15 Eagle assigned to the 71st Fighter Squadron, 1st Fighter Wing from Langley AFB, Virginia, on patrol in the skies over the East Coast. *USAF photograph/Staff Sargent Samuel Rogers*

The F-15 Eagle can carry a mixed combination of newer and more effective air-to-air missiles: AIM-7F/M Sparrow, AIM-120 AMRAAM, AIM-9L/M Sidewinder, and an air-to-air combination of 4 AIM-9 Sidewinder and 4 AIM-20 AMRAAM.

For the United States Air Force to maintain dominance over potential adversaries, the F-15 had to embrace emerging technologies that enhance its ability to survive in today's air combat environment. Improvements in the original F-15A/B variants led to the development of the F-15E Strike Eagle and the F-15SE Silent Eagle.

The F-15 Eagle made its maiden flight on 27 July 1972, but would not enter service with the Air Force until 9 January 1976. The F-15 has been the unrivaled master of the skies since its arrival in fighter squadrons of the United States Air Force, and its strongest ally in the Middle East, the Zroa Ha' Avir Ve' Halalal (Israeli Air and Space Force). The Israelis

The GAU-4 6-barrel M61 20 mm rotary cannons are on the starboard side of the F-15 near the engine intake. To date, no American F-15 Eagle has been credited with an aerial victory using the M61. *Public Domain photo by KOMATTA*

The F-15C configured with a combination of 4 AIM-9M Sidewinder and 4 AIM-120B Slammer air-to-air missiles. *USAF photograph*

would prove the overwhelming air superiority of the Eagle between 7 and 11 June 1982, when the Double Tail Squadron decimated Syrian Air Force MiG-21s and MiG-23s in air-to-air combat over Lebanon.

First F-15C Baz Aerial Victories
The F-15C would claim its first aerial victory not with the USAF, but with the Israeli Air and Space Force. On 27 June 1979, while flying Baz 663, Maj. (later Brig. Gen.) Moshe Melnik would claim the first F-15C kill, downing a MiG-21 with a Rafael Python 3 air-to-air missile.

The iconic F-15A *Hamadlik* (Fire Igniter, No. 663) flown by Maj. Moshe Melnik on 27 June 1979 on static display. No. 663 not only claimed the first aerial victory for the F-15 Eagle, but also the first victory for the Python 3 air-to-air missile. *A. Dor Collection*

The Rafael Advance Defense System Python 3 evolved from the Shafrif (Dragonfly) air-to-air missile. The Python 3 first appeared in 1959 with the IDF/AF. This Python 3 is attached to the port side wing of Baz No. 957 *Markia Shchakim* (Sky Blazer), credited to date with five aerial victories.

The F-15 Eagle in USAF service claimed its first aerial combat victory during the Gulf War. On 17 January 1991, Capt. Jon "JB" Kelk of the 33rd Tactical Fighter Wing (TFW) / 58th Tactical Fighter Squadron (TFS), call sign Pennzoil 63, downed an Iraqi MiG-29 in F-15C tail number 85-0125 with an AIM-7 Sparrow air-to-air missile.

With the F-15 solidly established as the Air Force's premier air superiority fighter, the search for an equally dominant multi-role fighter was on. On 20 January 1974, the General Dynamics F-16 Fighting Falcon conducted its first flight. The Falcon would not enter service until its introduction on 17 August 1978. The F-16 was originally designed as a day fighter, but quickly evolved into a successful all-weather multi-role aircraft.

Tail No. 85-0125, flown by Capt. Jon "JB" Kelk during his MiG-29 mission, taken in 1989 at Eglin AFB. Capt. Kelk has been credited with the first USAF aerial victories in the F-15C. *J. Geer Collection*

Members (Staff Sgts. Coronado and Hamabata) of the 154th Aircraft Maintenance Squadron, Hawaii Air National Guard loading AIM-7 Sparrows on an F-15 on 16 July 2006. At the time the 154th was participating in RIMPAC exercise 2006. *USAF photograph*

F-16A Netz No. 107 is by far the most outstanding example of the Falcon's multi-role capabilities. While in service with the IASF, F-16A Netz accumulated an impressive air-to-air combat record. Prior to being retired in February 2015, No. 107 stands on alert in a hardened shelter. Notice the combat record (6.5 roundels for aerial victories and a green triangle denoting participation in the OPERA raid) on the nose of the aircraft commemorating the jet's accomplishments. *O. Zidon Collection*

The General Dynamics (now Lockheed Martin) F-16 Falcon

The F-16 Fighting Falcon is a single-seat, single-engine multi-role fighter. When first introduced on 17 August 1978, the F-16 was designed as a day fighter, but would evolve into a superior all-weather multi-role combat aircraft. Since its first flight on 20 January 1974 with the United States Air Force, the Falcon may well be the world's most prolific fighter, with over 2,000 in service deployed with twenty-five other countries.

Like the F-15, the F-16 was born out of the Air Force's experience during the Vietnam War, which revealed not only the need for a pure dogfighter (F-15 Eagle), but a strong, lightweight fighter. General Dynamics Corporation was picked over four other companies to design and produce a new lightweight fighter that could carry out the air-to-ground and air-to-air mission.

General Dynamics' design of the new lightweight fighter known as the F-16 Fighting Falcon incorporated many features, including a frameless bubble canopy for better all-around visibility, a seat reclined 30 degrees to reduce g-forces on the pilot, an internal M61 Vulcan cannon, and 11 hard points for mounting external weapons and other mission equipment. The F-16 also possesses an outstanding turn and acceleration rate that enhances its survivability in battle.

F-16s from the 388th Fighter Wing, 12th Air Force, Hill AFB, Utah, over the desert in the Middle East. On the wing tips are AIM-120s. The 335 lb. missile is equipped with a 500 lb. high explosive blast-fragmentation warhead. *USAF photograph/Master Sgt. A. Dunaway*

The First F-16 Falcon (Netz) Aerial Victories

The Falcon would claim its first aerial combat victory not with the USAF, but with the IASF. On 28 April 1981, Dubi Yoffe, while flying F-16A Netz No. 126, engaged and destroyed a Syrian Mi-8 helicopter with its 20 mm 6-barrel Vulcan cannon. On 14 July 1981, Amir Nachumi, an Israeli F-16 pilot with the Knights of the North Squadron, would claim the first fixed wing "kill" when he downed a Syrian MiG-21 with a single AIM-9L Sidewinder air-to-air missile. Capt. Gary "Nordo" North (USAF) claimed a MiG-25 on 27 December 1992, with the new AIM-120 air-to-air missile that has become a force multiplier with as many as twenty-seven foreign air forces.

Since October 1981, despite its size the F-16 Falcon has proven itself to be in almost continuous combat operation somewhere in the world and are now engaged in Operation INHERENT RESOLVE against the Islamic State (ISIS) in Iraq and Syria, with Falcons from twenty-three countries participating.

The Zora HaVir Vehalalal (Israeli Air and Space Force) was first to introduce the F-16A Netz and F-16C/D Barak into combat in the Baqaa Valley, Lebanon. On 9 June 1982, the Israelis launched Operation MOLE CRICKET 19 against a Syrian network of overlapping surface-to-air missile targets in the Baqaa Valley. Israel has been in a perpetual state of war against Hezbollah, Hamas, the Palestine Liberation Organization (PLO), Syria, and Iran since its inception in 1948.

An F-16 from the 52nd Wing, today operating in the "Wild Weasel" role (suppression of enemy air defenses). Here the Falcon is configured with AIM-120s on its wingtips, AIM-9 Sidewinders on stations 2 and 8, an AGM-88 HARM starboard side, and Shrike anti-radiation missiles portside. *USAF photograph*

CHAPTER 3
CHEL HA' AVIR—ISRAELI DEFENSE FORCE/AIR FORCE

ISAF coat of arms

Middle East

The Chel Ha' Avir (Israeli Defense Force/Air Force) was officially formed on 28 May 1948, shortly after Israel declared statehood. Most of the fighter pilots of the new Chel Ha' Avir (IDF/AF) were ex-WWII volunteers. The fledgling IDF/AF was mostly comprised of obsolete WWII aircraft like the Supermarine Spitfire (approximately 62) and the Czechoslovak-built Messerchmitt Bf-109 Avira S-199. The IDF/AF initiated combat operations on 29 May 1948, when it launched four newly arrived S-199s (Sakeen, or Knife) flown by Lou Lenart, Modi Alone, Ezer Weizman, and Eddie Cohen against Egyptian forces near Isdud, in the northern part of the Gaza district. The attack was not without cost to the Israelis, who lost two of their S-199s and, more importantly to the Israelis, the loss of South African-born Messerschmitt pilot Eddie Cohen, who was shot down and listed as killed in action. Eddie Cohen thus became the first person listed on the Roll of Honour for the IDF/AF.

The first aerial combat victories claimed by Chel Ha' Avir came on 3 June 1948, when Modi Alone, flying an Avia 199 (tail or side No. D.112) downed two converted Egyptian DC-3s. The DC-3s had just completed a bombing raid on Tel Avia when Alone engaged them with cannon fire, sending both to the desert floor. As the war continued, the IDF/AF began to demonstrate its ability, gaining air superiority over the combined Arab air forces. This was truly illustrated on 8 June 1948, when for the first time an Israeli aircraft flown by Gideon Lichtaman engaged and downed an Egyptian Spitfire in a dogfight.

By the end of the war in 1949, the IDF/AF had established total air supremacy in the airspace over Israel with the infusion of new weapon systems like the Boeing B-17, de Havilland Mosquitoes, and P-51 Mustangs. Even with more and newer weapons, it has always been the men and women of the IDF/AF that have made the difference in battle.

Retired Aluf Mishne (Col.) Giora "Hawkeye" Epstein served in the Israeli Defense Force/Air Force 1956–1998. During his career in the IDF/AF he is credited with engaging and destroying 17 enemy aircraft in aerial combat. Col. Epstein is posing next to Nesher No. 159, clearly marked with 12 MiG kills all credited to Col. Epstein. *P. Mersky Collection*

Forged from many wars and countless attacks by its neighbors, Israel has built and maintained one of the world's most powerful air forces. The Chel Ha' Avir is today known as the Zroa Ha' Avir Ve' Halalal (Israel Air and Space Force). The IASF can claim more jet aces than any modern air force in the world; among them is retired IAF Reserve Col. Giora Even (Epstein), who is the world's leading jet ace, with seventeen confirmed aerial victories. During the Yom Kippur War he shot down twelve Egyptian aircraft—eight in just twenty-six hours.

The air battles flown by the delta wing Mirage and Neshers of the Israeli Air and Space Force against Egyptians, Syrians, Jordanians, Libyans, and even Russian and North Korean pilots are numerous. The Mirage, Nesher, and a mixed force of attack aircraft in the IASF have flown their last combat missions in the simmering cauldron known as the Middle East.

The Six Day War (5–10 June 1967), War of Attrition (1967–1970), and Yom Kippur War (6–25 October 1973) proved to Israeli air staff the need for a truly multi-role fighter. The Israeli Defense Force/Air Force command staff was brutally honest with itself about their Arab enemies' capabilities and the IDF/AF's own shortcomings. The Dassault Mirage III's and the Nesher's combat history have been widely documented and intensely researched as MiG killers, but their ability to put bombs on target has always been quite limited.

During the early to mid-'60s, the Israeli government approached the United States numerous times, attempting to obtain the combat proven F-4 Phantom II. Israelis were convinced the F-4 Phantom II, with its advantage in technology and enhanced development of newer weapon systems, would be the multi-role fighter they needed for the modern battlefield in the Middle East.

Under extraordinarily stressful negotiations the United States and Israel finally came to an agreement in which the United States would export to Israel 50 F-4E Phantom IIs. The sale could not have come at a more opportune time for the Israelis; in January 1968, Gamal Abdel Nasser commenced the War of Attrition against Israel.

The first of the F-4E series were introduced by the IDF/AF in September 1969, with No. 201 Squadron, known as "The One" Squadron. In less than seventy days, the Kurnass was flying in combat with the IDF/AF and would claim its first air-to-air victory on 11 November 1969; Shamuel Hertz (pilot) and Menachem Eini (weapon system officer, WSO) engaged and destroyed an Egyptian MiG-21 with an air-to-air missile.

The F-4E Kurnass in service with the Chel Ha' Avir (IDF/AF) and later Zroa Ha' Avir Ve' Halalal (Israeli Air and Space Force) saw extensive combat during many Arab-Israeli conflicts. During its thirty-five years of service, the Kurnass was capable of fulfilling the multi-fighter role the IDF/AF so desperately needed in the mid-'60s. The F-4s of the IASF were mainly committed to air-to-ground, but also proved quite adept at performing air-to-air missions in the skies of the Middle East. F4-E Kurnass squadrons claimed 116.5 aerial victories November 1969–June 1982. The air-to-air kill ratio of the Kurnass F-4E is most remarkable when you consider the Sledgehammer was deployed by the Israelis essentially

The king of all F-4E Phantom MiG killers (No. 109) while serving with the IASF. The iconic MiG killer claimed seven aerial victories. Unfortunately, this historic aircraft was lost as the result of a midair collision with an A-4 of the IASF. *A. Dor Collection*

The all-time leading Kurnass MiG killer is No. 109, with seven confirmed kills. Israeli airmen stand proudly next to 109, with seven kill markings visible on the nose of the aircraft. *O. Zidon Collection*

as a fighter-bomber, yet established an outstanding kill-to-loss exchange rate in air-to-air combat over Arab air forces. Sources (*Israeli F-4 Phantom II Aces*) confirm that November–September 1973, the kill / loss rate was 25 to 1, during the Yom Kippur War 85 to 5, and from December 1972 to June 1982 6.5 to 0.

The always volatile political climate in the Middle East and the realization that Arab countries were obtaining more sophisticated weapons weighed heavy in the minds of military leaders in Israel. Increased losses in aircraft and aircrews proved to be extraordinarily stressful for the Israeli Air and Space Force. The Yom Kippur (Atonement Day) War lasted only 19 days (6–25 October 1973), but was without a doubt an extremely painful experience for the Israelis. Unofficial reports suggest Israel may have lost approximately 103 combat aircraft destroyed and another 200 damaged.

As early as 1969, the IDF/AF began the search to replace the F-4Es in its inventory. It was quite clear they would need an aircraft a generation ahead of its enemies to maintain air dominance in the Middle East. The Israeli Ministry of Defense requested a detailed outline of operational requirements from the air staff for the successor to the multi-role F-4E Kurnass. A key requirement with the IASF was aircraft would have the versatility to adapt to the air-to-air and air-to-ground roles.

In June 1974, the Israelis approached the United States to obtain a fourth generation fighter that would satisfy their real world concerns. The Israelis and the United States entered into an agreement wherein the Israelis would be allowed to evaluate head-to-head the McDonnell Douglas F-15 Eagle and the Grumman F-14 Tomcat.

With the evaluation agreement in place, the Israelis sent an impressive team of pilots to the United States. Leading the team was Ammon Arad, a former Kurnass pilot and commander of one of Israel's Kurnass squadrons. The remainder of the evaluation team (Israel Baharav, Omri Afek, and Assaf Ben-Num) were a collection of some of Israel's most outstanding fast jet pilots. Between them the team was credited with no less than twenty-four aerial combat victories. Baharav (12 victories) and Ben-Nun (5 victories) were certified aces.

When the dust settled and the test team presented their unanimous decision, the McDonnell Douglas F-15 Eagle was found the best air superiority platform for the present and future needs of the Chel Ha' Avir.

Double Tail Squadron and Spearhead Squadron

F-15A/C/D Baz

During the evaluation, the Eagle and Tomcat were put through rigorous testing to establish their versatility in maneuverability, weapons systems, flight characteristics, air superiority, and their ability to deal with low and slow (helicopters) and high and fast (Foxbat MiG-25s) air threats.

The Zroa Ha' Avir Ve' Halalal (IASF) has always been very security conscious regarding details of its fighter squadrons. Information on locations and disbursement of fighter squadrons and aircraft has always been jealously guarded. Information in the public record suggests Israel presently has three operational F-15 squadrons: No. 133 Squadron (Double Tail Squadron), Tel Nof Air Base; No. 106 Squadron (Spearhead Squadron), Tel Nof Air Base; and No. 69 Squadron (Hammer Squadron), Hatzerim Air Base.

On 28 November 1976, Double Tail was the first F-15 squadron activated at Tel Nof Air Force Base, near Rehovot, Israel. The first F-15A/B models began arriving on 10 December 1976, and upon arrival were renamed the Baz, while later F-15C/D models were named Baz (Akef, or Buzzard).

On 6 June 1982, Double Tail Squadron was joined by Spearhead Squadron at Tel Nof Air Base. The activation of Spearhead Squadron brought the total number of combat ready F-15s to approximately 40–50.

Double Tail Squadron Claims First MiG Kill

On 11 March 1978, Palestinian Al Fatah terrorists launched one of the deadliest assaults on Israeli civilians, killing thirty-six passengers on a bus traveling near Maagan Michael. In response to the terrorist attack Israel launched Operation LITANI. During the heightened tension the Double Tail Squadron was tasked with Combat Air Patrol (CAP) missions, protecting Israeli aircraft engaged in air-to-ground missions over Lebanon. On 27 June 1979, a routine CAP mission over Sidon and Tyre, Lebanon, was challenged by Syrian Air Force MiG-21s.

Israeli CAP flights Groom and Thames were vectored by ground control to intercept 6 MIG-21s launched against attacking Israeli aircraft. Groom flight consisted of 4 F-15As led by Benjamin Zin; Groom 2, 3, and 4 were Moshe Melnik, Eitan Ben-Eliyahu, and Joel Feldschuh. Thames flight was a mixture of F-15As and Kfir C-2s and was led by Yoram Peled; 2, 3, and 4 were Guy Golan, Ben Amitay, and Shay Eshel.

During the engagement Groom 2 (Melnik) spotted a pair of Syrian MiGs about to cross his flight path from the right. Groom 2 armed a Python 3, and once all firing parameters were met the missile was launched. The Python air-to-air missile exploded upon impact, totally destroying the MiG. Moshe Melnik's (Groom 2) kill was the first aerial combat victory for the F-15 (No. 663), as well as the first kill for the Israeli produced Python 3 air-to-air missile.

As the air battle between the Israeli F-15 Baz and Syrian MiG-21 Fishbeds continued, Groom 3 (No. 689, Ben-Eliyahu) and Groom 4 (No. 704, Feldsho) would engage, fire on, and destroy a MiG. Yoram Peled, flying lead in (No. 672) Thames flight, also downed a Syrian MiG with an AIM-9G air-to-air missile.

F-16A/B Netz and Barak Join Knights of the Orange Tail Squadron

During the 1980s, the IASF began receiving the F-16 Falcon to augment their Baz squadrons. The first Falcons were received at Hatzerim AFB and assigned to the Knights of the Orange Tail Squadron. The F-16s in the IASF carry the nicknames Netz (Sparrowhawk) and Barak (Lightning). The F-16 has been mainly deployed as a strike aircraft with the IASF, but the F-16 has surely proven itself a dual purpose aircraft.

By April 1981, the F-16A/B Netz had been integrated into operational units of the IASF and was actively involved in combat operations. On 28 April 1981, Dubi Yoffe (in 126), flying with the First Jet Squadron, recorded the first air-to-air success over the Baqaa Valley when he downed a Syrian (SyAAF) Mi-8 helicopter. On 14 July 1981, Amir Nahumi (in 112) from the Knights of the North squadron would claim the first fixed-wing kill, downing a MiG-21 with an AIM-9L Sidewinder air-to-air missile.

Double Tail Squadron Kills Four MiG-21s in 77 Seconds

Despite the loss of four MiGs during June 1979, the Syrians continued their aggressive overflights of Lebanon. They began to deploy MiG-23MS Flogger-Gs in an attempt to intercept Israeli RF-4E reconnaissance aircraft. The Russian supplied swing-wing Flogger engaged an Israeli RF-4E, firing at least three air-to-air missiles at it. Fortunately, the RF-4E evaded the missiles and returned safely to Israel.

Syrian Air Force attempts to intercept Israeli reconnaissance and strike aircraft continued to increase in intensity. In September 1979, the Double Tail Squadron set into motion a plan to intercept and engage Syrian MiGs as they attempted to attack Israeli aircraft.

On 24 September 1979, six F-15s from Double Tail Squadron launched from Tel Nof Air Base and were engaged by an equal number of MiG-21s that had scrambled to intercept them. Within 77 seconds from the time the two forces met, four of the six Syrian MiG-21s were shot down with no Israeli aircraft lost or damaged: the first MiG was downed by Avner Naveh (in 695) with a single Python 3 air-to-air missile; the second MiG was claimed by Dedi Rosenthal (in 676) with an AIM-7F; the third MiG fell to Relik Shafir with an AIM-9 AAM; and the fourth MiG-21 was downed by Naveh (in 695) with 20 mm cannon fire.

From 24 August 1980 until 13 February 1981, pilots from Double Tail Squadron would claim and be credited with three additional Syrian MiG-21s and one MiG-25 Foxbat. On the 24th, Ilan Margalit (in 696) was flying in the number two position of a mixed CAP flight (2 F-15s and 2 Kfir Cs) when he spotted four Syrian MiG-21s attempting to intercept and engage an RF-4E reconnaissance aircraft. Margalit, who was targeting two of the MiGs, was able to lock on to one of the MiGs with an AIM-7F radar missile. The missile tracked directly to the Syrian MiG and caused a violent explosion upon impact, totally destroying the MiG.

On 31 December 1980, Israeli aircraft continued their air assault in southern Lebanon. Yair Rachmilevic (in 646) and Yoav Stern (in 695)—F-15 Baz pilots from Double Tail Squadron—were part of a mixed CAP (2 F-15s and 2 F-4Es) formation protecting strike aircraft. The CAP flight was vectored to intercept a flight of four MiG-21s inbound, heading toward the Israeli strike aircraft. Rachmievic, upon discovering the attacking MiG, armed one of his Python 3 air-to-air missiles, received a good tone indicating the missile had locked on to the target, and fired. A second MiG was also destroyed, but there is some question as to who downed it; the second kill is listed as a shared victory between Yoav Stern of Double Tail Squadron and the F-4E Kurnass aircrew of Ran Granot and Evi Erlich from 119 Squadron.

First MiG-25 Foxbat Kill

The Soviet Union has long been the major weapons supplier for the Syrian Air Force. With continued poor showing of the Mikoyan-Gurevich MiG-21 Fishbed against the Israeli F-15 Baz over Lebanon, the Soviets began to supply the Syrians with the advanced MiG-23 Flogger and the supersonic MiG-25 Foxbat in hopes of overcoming Israeli F-15 air dominance.

On 13 February 1981, the Israelis sent two RF-4Es on a somewhat deceptive reconnaissance mission over southern Lebanon in an attempt to entice the Syrians to respond by launching their new MiG-25s. The Israelis' highly effective COMINT- SIGINT units detected the launch of two MiG-25s. The CAP formations protecting the RF-4Es were ordered to intercept and engage the Syrian MiGs. Benny Zinker (in 672), commanding officer of Double Tail Squadron, was leading the CAP formation. While in the area of Kiryat Shmona, near the Lebanese border, he engaged a MiG and fired one of his AIM-7F radar AAM. Within moments of the launch he witnessed a large explosion. The kill was quickly confirmed, but the type of MiG downed would not be established for some time; it was eventually identified as a Foxbat.

On 29 July 1981, a second Syrian MiG-25 was engaged by Shaul Simon (in 673) of Double Tail Squadron, who downed the Foxbat with an AIM-7F air-to-air missile.

CHAPTER 4
OPERATION PEACE FOR GALILEE

Mivtsa Shlom HaGalil or Mivtsa Sheleg

During the summer of 1982, terrorist gunmen (Hussein Ghassan Said, Marwan al-Banna, and Nawaf al-Rosan) from the Abu Nidals organization—also known as Black June and the Arab Revolutionary Brigade—attempted to assassinate Israel's ambassador to the United Kingdom Shlomo Argov. The ambassador was badly wounded on 3 June 1982, when he was shot in the head as he entered his car after a banquet in England.

Tensions continued to escalate when Israeli intelligence discovered Syria had moved surface-to-air missile (SAM) batteries into the Baqaa Valley, in eastern Lebanon. Defense Minister Ariel Sharon acted quickly on 6 June 1982, directing Israeli Defense Forces to invade southern Lebanon behind massive air strikes dubbed Mivtza Artzav Tsha-Esreh (Operation MOLE CRICKET 19).

Operation MOLE CRICKET 19 was launched on 9 June 1982 against Syrian air defenses in the Baqaa Valley. The Israeli Air Force unleashed a devastating air campaign to suppress soviet-built SAM batteries deployed by the Syrians. During MOLE CRICKET 19, using innovative air tactics and the most modern technology, Israel totally destroyed 17 of 19 SAM sites by the end of the day. F-4E Kurnass armed with AGM-78 and AGM-45 anti-radiation missiles carried out the bulk of air-to-ground attacks, devastating the SAM sites. The Syrians responded by launching about 100 aircraft, mostly MiG-21s, MiG-23s, and Su-20s. Israeli F-15 Bazs and F-16 Netzs directed by E-2C AWACS successfully intercepted the fast approaching SyAAF MiGs. When the air battle was over, the SyAAF had sustained significant losses. By the time an American brokered cease-fire went into effect at 6:00 a.m. on 10 June, Israeli F-15 Baz and F-16 Netz had engaged the Syrian Air Force in the biggest air battle since the Korean War. Israeli pilots and aircraft totally outclassed their Syrian counterparts by destroying approximately 82 to 90 enemy aircraft in air combat without a single loss.

Operation MIVTZA ARTZAV TSHA-ESREH was the first time in history Western forces were able to deliver a deadly blow to a Soviet integrated air defense system (IADS). The Israeli F-4E Kurnass and F-16 Netz destroyed the Soviet surface-to-air missile sites consisting of SA-2 (Guideline), SA-3 (GOA), and SA-6 (Gainful) missiles. Israeli after-action reports indicated Syrians fired upward of 57 SAMs during Operation MOLE CRICKET 19 with absolutely no effect.

The overwhelming defeat of the Soviet integrated air defense system (IADS) and the subsequent destruction of over 90 Syrian Air Force aircraft sent shock waves reverberating from the Middle East to the Kremlin. The destruction was so complete that Soviet political and military leadership feared NATO might do the same in eastern Europe.

The most stunning achievement during Operation PEACE for GALILEE (Mole Cricket 19) was the Israelis' ability to destroy Russian and Syrian surface-to-air missile (SAM) sites in the Baqaa Valley within a matter of hours. The battle area, both air and ground, was totally dictated by the Israelis utilizing decoys, anti-radiation missiles, and several classified locally developed weapon systems.

All attempts by the Syrian Air Force to disrupt Operation Mole Cricket 19 by engaging the Israelis met with total disaster; dozens of Syrian MiG-21s and MiG-23s were destroyed in mass dogfights without a single Israeli loss.

CHAPTER 5
F-15 Baz Baptism of Fire

Aerial Combat Victories of the F-15 Baz

Since its arrival in Israel (December 1970) and deployment with Double Tail and Spearhead Squadrons, the F-15C/D Baz was able to command the skies of the Middle East. During 27 June 1979 to 19 November 1985, the F-15s of the Israeli Air and Space Force (IASF) have been credited with no less than 52 confirmed aerial victories. Two MiG-23 Floggers have been classified as squadron kills, and as such the pilots or pilot could not be positively identified.

When war broke out in June 1982, the Syrian Air Force attempted to challenge the IDF/AF in the skies over Lebanon. The attempt proved to be a total catastrophe for the SyAAF. The kill ratio in June 1982 (33 to 0) for Israeli F-15s against the Syrian Air Force's MiG-21s, MiG-23s, and MiG-25s is overwhelmingly in favor of the F-15 Baz. The fourth generation Baz is now serving as the primary interceptor, and along with the uncompromising demand for perfection the IASF has established, for the foreseeable future Israel will continue to be the most dominant air force in the Middle East.

During Operation PEACE for GALILEE the world's first and only F-15 ace would emerge. On 10 June 1982, then Maj. Avner Naveh would claim two MiG-23s and a SyAAF MiG-21. These three aerial victories, along with confirmed kills on 24 September 1979 and 19 November 1985, would bring his total kills to 6.5.

Appearing in chronological order by date are the F-15 Baz MiG killers of the IASF from 27 June 1979 to 19 November 1985.

27 June 1979
F-15A, No. 663
Hamadlik / Fire Igniter
Double Tail Squadron
Maj. Moshe Melnik

F-15A-MC 76-1508 No. 663—aircraft destroyed: 1 MiG-21; weapon: Python 3 AAM. The IASF radio traffic was full of excited pilots shouting "hipalti" ("I scored a kill!"). Once Double Tail pilots were on the ground and everyone had told of their kills, Maj. Melnik uttered one sentence that everyone still remembers, "Say what you will—I was the first."

Prior to 27 June 1979, Maj. Melnik was no stranger to aerial combat. After graduating from flying school (class 54) in 1967, he flew the A-4 Ahit (Eagle) and F-4E Kurnass (Sledgehammer) in squadron service. Flying with No. 119 Squadron during the War of Attrition and Yom Kipper War, Maj. Melnik earned ace status on 23 October 1973, while flying in Kurnass No. 162.

Moshe Melnik would retire from the Israeli Air and Space Force (IASF) as a brigadier general. The brigadier ended his flying career with 8.5 aerial victories, having been credited with two additional Baz kills on 8 and 9 June 1982 (in 802).

Baz 663 taxiing past the photographer. Painted on the fuselage in Hebrew is the nickname *Hamadlik* (Fire Igniter). Also clearly visible is the MiG kill marking denoting the historic first aerial victory by Maj. Melnik on 27 June 1979. Not only did the major claim the first victory in the world for the American built fighter, but also the first kill for the Rafael Python 3 AAM. Legend has it that while in St. Louis, Missouri, visiting McDonnell Douglas, Maj. Melnik told his host he would be the first pilot to make a kill in the F-15. *O. Zidon Collection*

Baz 404 sits in a shelter protecting IASF personnel from the blazing desert heat while they tend to the MiG killer. This aircraft's tail number was changed from 704 to 404 sometime in the mid-'80s. The F-15B still proudly displays two markings for kills on 27 June 1979 and 11 June 1982. Baz 404 wears the tail markings of the Twin Tail Squadron. *O. Zidon Collection*

27 June 1979
11 June 1982
F-15B, No. 404
Hetz Mi Keshet / Arrow
**   from Bow**
Double Tail Squadron
Maj. Yoel Feldsho
Capt.-Maj. Shaul Simon
Capt. Amir Hodorov

F-15B-16-MC 76-1524 No. 404—aircraft destroyed: 2 MiG-21s; weapon: AIM-7F Sparrow AAM / Python 3 AAM. On 27 June 1979, Maj. Yoel Feldsho, flying with Double Tail Squadron out of Tel-Nof Air Base, downed a Syrian MiG-21 before the pilot was able to obtain missile lock on Maj. Melnik. Maj. Feldsho was able to obtain radar lock on the Syrian MiG with an AIM-7F Sparrow missile and successfully launched the AIM-7F, which tracked to the enemy aircraft and detonated, destroying the MiG.

On 11 June 1982, Tail No. 404 claimed its second Syrian MiG-21 when Capt.-Maj. Shaul Simon and Capt. Amir Hodorov engaged, fired on, and destroyed an enemy MiG-21 Fishbed with a Python 3. This would be the second documented aerial victory for Baz 404.

Baz 672 taxiing at an air base in Israel. It is clear by the blacked out squadron emblem on the tail of the aircraft that the censor did not want the squadron identified when this photo was taken. This historic Baz was lost in 1981, in a midair collision with another F-15 (684); both pilots were killed. *O. Zidon Collection*

27 June 1979
13 February 1981
F-15A, No. 672
Tornado
Double Tail Squadron
Maj. Yoram Peled
Lt. Col. Benny Zinker

F-15A-17-MC 76-1511 No. 672—aircraft destroyed: 1 MiG-21; 1 MiG-25; weapon: AIM-9G Sidewinder AAM / AIM-7F Sparrow AAM. Maj. Yoram Peled was on a low CAP mission when he downed a Syrian MiG-21 with an AIM-9G air-to-air missile. Peled had locked on to the MiG and fired just seconds before another Baz pilot was about to engage the same MiG. During the short air battle on 27 June Double Tail Squadron F-15s claimed four Syrian MiGs.

On 13 February 1981, Double Tail Squadron CO Lt. Col. Benny Zinker was flying as flight leader of a CAP tasked with protecting a photographic reconnaissance mission when they were contacted by ground control that Syrian fighters were being vectored to intercept the IASF RF-4. The RF-4E mission was aborted and the crew was sent home.

Zinker was in the area of the Lebanese/Israeli border when he engaged the enemy aircraft at twenty-five miles. The Baz pilot launched two AIM-7F radar missiles and was about to launch a third when he witnessed a huge explosion. At the time of the kill Lt. Col. Zinker was not sure what type of aircraft he had destroyed. It would be confirmed some weeks later by Israeli intelligence that he had destroyed a Syrian MiG-25P.

The nickname *Boomerang* in Hebrew of No. 689 is captured while taxiing out for a training mission. The aircraft is marked with two aerial victories: one is the MiG-21 kill of 27 June 1979 credited to Lt. Col. Eitan Ben-Eliyahu, while the second may very well be a squadron kill. *O. Zidon Collection*

27 June 1979
F-15A, No. 689
Boomerang
Double Tail Squadron
Lt. Col. Eitan Ben-Eliyahu

F-15A-18-MC 76-1518 No. 689—aircraft destroyed: 1 MiG-21; weapon: 20 mm cannon. Lt. Col. Eitan Ben-Eliyahu had locked on to a MiG-21 and was about to engage when it was hit by a Sidewinder AAM missile fired by Lt. Col. Zinker. A second Syrian MiG presented itself, and the former commanding officer of Double Tail Squadron Ben-Eliyahu locked on to the MiG and fired a burst from his 20 mm cannon, resulting in the demise of the Syrian MiG.

With four SyAAF MiG-21 kills credited to No. 695, it sits in a shelter armed with air-to-air missiles. The four kills were made from 1979 to 1982, with the last kill in June 1982. There is presently an F-15 Baz on display at the IASF Museum with No. 695 marked with four aerial victories. This aircraft is not the original 695, which is still in service with the IASF. *O. Zidon Collection*

24 September 1979
31 December 1980
9 June 1982
F-15A, No. 695
Ha Kochav / The Star
Double Tail Squadron
Maj. Avner Naveh
Maj. Avner Naveh
Capt. Oran Hampel

F-15A-18-MC 76-1521 No. 695—aircraft destroyed: 4 MiG-21s; weapons: Python 3 AAM / AIM-7F Sparrow AAM / 20 mm cannon. During September 1979, a Syrian MiG-23 Flogger launched a number of air-to-air missiles in an attempt to shoot down an IASF RF-4E. The Phantom II was able to fend off the Flogger attack and return home safely.

In retaliation for the aggressive action of the Syrians over Lebanon the Israelis set a trap to engage the SyAAF MiGs. The IASF launched two sections of F-15s: one section was designed to lure the MiGs into action, while the second flight of four Baz from Double Tail Squadron would do the interception.

The SyAAF scrambled six MiG-21s and in just over a minute, four of the MiGs were shot down by IASF F-15s. Maj. Avner Naveh downed the first MiG with an air-to-air Python 3 missile. He claimed a second MiG-21 kill with his internal 20 mm cannon.

On 31 December 1980, Capt. Yoav Stern claimed the third kill credited to Baz No. 695 when he downed a SyAAF MiG-21 with a Python 3 missile. The fourth kill for this F-15 was credited to Capt. Oran Hampel, who added a MiG-21 on 9 June 1982. Hampel brought down his MiG with an AIM-7F Sparrow missile.

Baz 676 was the aircraft flown by Capt. Rosenthal of Double Tail Squadron on 24 September 1979, when he shot down his MiG-21 over southern Lebanon. Just five days after the MiG-21 kill, this aircraft was lost during a bad weather landing at Tel Nof Air Base. Pilot Guy Golan was killed. Here 676 is captured landing after a CAP configured with air-to-air missiles. *O. Zidon Collection*

24 September 1979
F-15A, No. 676
No Name Given
Double Tail Squadron
Capt. Dedi Rosenthal

F-15A-17-MC 76-1513 No. 676—aircraft destroyed: 1 MiG-21; weapon: AIM-7F Sparrow AAM. Capt. Dedi Rosenthal was part of an ambush flight that shot down four out of six Syrian MiG-21s on 24 September 1979. Shortly after flight leader Maj. Avner Naveh shot down his first of two MiGs, Rosenthal locked on to one of the enemy MiGs with a radar guided Sparrow missile and once all firing parameters were satisfied pulled the trigger, launching the missile. The missile proved to be a direct hit, resulting in destruction of another SyAAF MiG.

F-15A No. 692 from Double Tail Squadron was flown on 24 September 1979 by Relik Shafir when he downed a Syrian MiG-21 Fishbed with a single AIM-9 Sidewinder. Baz 692 carries the nickname *Galaxy* in Hebrew on its nose just above its number. *O. Zidon Collection*

24 September 1979
F-15A, No. 692
Galaxy
Double Tail Squadron
Relik Shafir

F-15A-18-MC 76-1520 No. 692—aircraft destroyed: 1 MiG-21; weapon: AIM-9G Sidewinder AAM. The fourth MiG kill of 24 September 1979 was credited to Relik Shafir of Double Tail Squadron. The ambush on 24 September 1979, like the air battle on 27 June 1979, was designed by the IASF in response to aggressive action of the SyAAF over Lebanon. The defensive air operations conducted by the IASF were intended to deter SyAAF operations over Lebanon.

Haziz (Firecracker, No. 696) is preparing to launch from what appears to be a forward operating location. The solitary MiG kill symbol on the nose of the aircraft denotes Maj. Ilan Margalit's aerial victory over SyAAF pilot Nabil Girgis, who managed to eject and survive the engagement. *Y. Lapid Collection*

24 August 1980
F-15A, No. 696
Haziz / Firecracker
Double Tail Squadron
Maj. Ilan Margalit

F-15A-18-MC 76-1522 No. 696—aircraft destroyed: 1 MiG-21; weapon: AIM-7F Sparrow AAM. On 24 August 1980, the IASF and SyAAF again engaged in air combat over Lebanon. IASF RF-4Es were conducting a photo reconnaissance mission when the Syrians launched a flight of four MiGs to intercept the Israeli reconnaissance aircraft.

The IASF CAP tasked to protect the RF-4Es was vectored to intercept the approaching MiG-21s.

Maj. Ilan Margalit visually acquired one of the MiG-21s heading directly at him. The aircraft were on a collision course when Margalit unleashed one of his AIM-7 missiles. The missile tracked directly to the target and in an instant the MiG-21 was seen to explode and disintegrate.

F-15A Baz No. 646 in the tail markings of Double Tail Squadron. No. 646 was one of the FSD airframes supplied to the IASF in December 1976. Even though 646 is credited with four aerial victories, the aircraft was not chosen to undergo AUP upgrading due to age of the airframe. *O. Zidon Collection*

31 December 1980
9 June 1982
9 June 1982
11 June 1982
F-15A, No. 646
Ra'am / Thunder
Double Tail Squadron
Capt. Yair Rachmilevic
Capt. Avi Maor

F-15A-6-MC 72-0118 No. 646—aircraft destroyed: 3 MiG-21s; 1 MiG-23: weapon: AIM-9G Sidewinder AAM / Python 3 AAM / 20 mm cannon. During November and December 1980, the IASF continued to attack PLO strongholds throughout Lebanon, particularly in the southern part of the country. On 31 December 1980, the SyAAF attempted to disrupt Israeli air operations by scrambling MiGs to intercept IASF fighter-bombers. Capt. Yair Rachmilevic was flying as part of a CAP protecting strike aircraft when he identified a Syrian MiG-21. He immediately engaged the SyAAF aircraft by launching three Python air-to-air missiles that tracked to the MiG. This kill was the tenth thus far for the F-15 Baz.

On 9 June 1982, Capt. Avi Maor was flying Baz 646 as part of a four-ship CAP when the flight intercepted two MiG-23 Floggers of the Syrian Air Force. The F-15 CAP flight took the Floggers under attack and downed both enemy aircraft. One of the Floggers was downed by a Python 3 launched by Maor. Maor observed the pilot under his chute shortly after the destruction of the MiG-23.

F-15 Baz No. 673 just touching down. The nickname in Hebrew is *Ha Oketz*, which translates in English to "The Sting." F-15 No. 673 is proudly wearing the markings of Double Tail Squadron. Note the smiling eagle's head on the inner surface of the vertical stabilizer. *O. Zidon Collection*

29 July 1981
F-15A, No. 673
Ha Oketz / The Sting
Double Tail Squadron
Maj. Shaul Simon

F-15A-17-MC 76-1512 No. 673—aircraft destroyed: 1 MiG-25; weapon: AIM-7F Sparrow AAM. On 29 July 1981, the IASF shot down a second MiG-25 attempting to engage an RF-4E on a reconnaissance overflight of Lebanon. The SyAAF had scrambled two MiG-21s and two MiG-25s that were vectored to intercept the Israeli RF-4E.

The Syrian aircraft were intercepted by F-15s from Double Tail Squadron. Capt. Maj. Shaul Simon visually acquired the Foxbats and once in range locked on with one of his radar guided AIM-7F air-to-air missiles. Once the weapon was on its way it tracked to the target and within seconds impacted with the MiG, totally destroying the aircraft.

Double MiG killer No. 658 (center) at Tel Nof Air Base on 24 April 2007, at an open house during the celebration of the 59th anniversary of Israel's Independence. *E. Eckstein Collection*

7 June 1982
9 June 1982
F-15A, No. 658
Typhoon
Double Tail Squadron
Maj. Ofer Lapidot
Capt. Gil Rapaport

F-15A-17-MC 76-1506 No. 658—aircraft destroyed: 2 MiG-23s; weapon: Python 3 AAM / AIM-7F Sparrow AAM. Maj. Ofer Lapidot was south of Beirut on CAP when his flight was vectored to intercept a flight of SyAAF aircraft that were a threat to IASF strike aircraft. Lapidot visually identified the enemy MiG-23s at approximately seven miles. Lapidot informed the flight he had positively identified the target and was locked on with a Sparrow missile. The missile launched but failed to track. Lapidot maneuvered into Python missile range and at a distance of approximately 1½ miles—well within visual range (WVR)—fired the missile. Lapidot did not observe the missile impact with the Russian built Flogger, but other members of his flight did see the kill and confirmed his victory.

On 9 June 1982, the SyAAF lost twenty-five aircraft to IASF fighters. Double Tail Squadron's F-15 pilots were credited with eleven of these kills. One of the eleven was by Baz pilot Capt. Gil Rapaport, who downed a MiG-23 with a radar guided Sparrow missile.

Baz No. 658 taking off from an unidentified location, though the background suggests the Ovda Valley, Negev Desert, home of Ovda Air Base. Ovda Air Base hosted the first Blue Flag exercises involving aircraft from the United States, Greece, and Italy. *A. Azar Zohar Collection*

39

Baz 957, in the markings of Spearhead Squadron, moments after liftoff heading for a training mission. Spearhead Squadron was established as the IASF's second F-15 squadron on 16 June 1982. It did not take long for the squadron to claim its first aerial victory. On 24 June 1982, the squadron was credited with the destruction of 2 MiG-23 Floggers. *O. Zidon Collection*

F-15D-28-MC 80-0133 No. 957—aircraft destroyed: 2 MiG-21s, 3 MiG-23s; weapon: AIM-7F Sparrow AAM / Python 3 AAM. On 8 June 1982, IASF strike aircraft launched an aggressive bombing campaign directed at Syrian troop concentrations in Lebanon. The IASF air strikes forced the SyAAF to generate a large number of combat sorties in an attempt to intercept Israeli aircraft. On 8 June, IASF AWACS aircraft and radar units detected SyAAF MiGs attacking IASF strike flights. F-15D pilot Capt. Shaul Schwartz and his navigator, Capt. Reuven Solan, were leading Palace flight when they were vectored by their ground controller to intercept the SyAAF MiGs.

Palace 01 acquired the enemy aircraft and visually identified it as a MiG-21. The MiG pilot attempted to evade Palace 01 and his wingman by maneuvering in a banking turn to the south in full afterburner. Schwartz fired a single Sparrow missile at the fleeing enemy fighter. The missile tracked true to the target and within seconds the MiG-21 exploded, falling to the ground in flames. Schwartz's wingman also claimed and was credited with a MiG-21 victory in the same engagement.

The ground war in the Lebanon Valley grew in intensity on 10 June 1982, particularly in the area south of the Beirut-Damascus highway. Israeli and Syrian ground troops were heavily engaged, forcing the SyAAF to switch air operations from air-to-air to air-to-ground.

IASF aircraft continued to provide CAPs for their attacking aircraft. During air operations on 10 June, Maj. Avner Naveh and his back seater, Capt. Michael Cohen, from Double Tail Squadron downed three Syrian MiGs, making Naveh and Cohen the first Baz pilots to claim three kills during a single intercept. Their first of three kills was two MiG-23 Floggers, followed by a MiG-21. The three aerial victories by Naveh made him the world's first F-15 ace.

On 19 November 1985, Yuval Ben-Dor and Ofer Paz, flying with Spearhead Squadron on a CAP in direct support of a reconnaissance flight over Lebanon, were vectored to intercept a flight of SyAAF Floggers. During the engagement their first attempt at taking out the enemy fighters with an AIM-7 failed. The CAP continued to maneuver into position. Once in position Ben-Dor selected a Python 3 air-to-air missile and fired. The missile tracked directly to the target and upon impact totally destroyed the Syrian fighter.

During May 1983, Baz 957 was involved in a DACT mission; during the mission Baz 957, piloted by Ziv Nadivi and his navigator Yehoar Gal, collided with an Israeli A-4 during a one-on-one engagement. The F-15 lost most of its right wing as a result. It has been described as an amazing feat of airmanship that the crew of the Baz were able to land the badly damaged aircraft at Ramon Air Base. The aircraft would eventually be repaired and return to service.

Baz No. 957 is on arrival in the Czech Republic on 22 September 2011. Baz No. 957 is one of the highest scoring MiG killers in the IASF with 5 confirmed aerial victories (2 MiG-21s and 3 MiG-23s). *R. Kolek Collection*

Baz 686 taxiing on the runway of an IASF air base after completing a quick reaction alert (QRA) or CAP mission. The aircraft is seen in the tail markings of Double Tail Squadron and heavily armed with AAMs. Seen on the vertical stabilizer is an oversize IASF badge and special emblem that adorned IASF aircraft during the 50th anniversary (Golden Jubilee) celebrations. *O. Zidon Collection*

8 June 1982
9 June 1982
F-15A, No. 686
Ha'Lohet / Burning Hot
Double Tail Squadron
Capt. Yoram Hoffman
Maj. Ronen Shapira

F-15A-18-MC 76-1517 No. 686—aircraft destroyed: 2 MiG-21s; weapon: AIM-7F Sparrow AAM / Python 3 AAM. On 8 June 1982, Capt. Yoram Hoffman was flying as Palace 02 when he located a low flying, fast moving target east of Beirut. He positively identified the target as a Syrian MiG-21 Fishbed. Hoffman obtained a radar lock on the Syrian jet and after satisfying launch requirements fired the missile. Hoffman's missile scored a direct hit on the enemy aircraft, destroying it on impact.

Maj. Ronen Shapira claimed his MiG kill during air operations the second day of the Lebanon War. While engaged in a CAP mission Shapira was in the awkward position of having a MiG-21 on his tail. The Baz pilot executed a low speed, high-G turn, enabling him to maneuver his aircraft into the six o'clock position of the MiG, whereupon he armed and fired an air-to-air missile. The missile launched, unfortunately failing to hit the target. A second missile was launched (Python 3) and this time the result was far different; it impacted and detonated, destroying the SyAAF MiG.

No. 818 parked in the hot sun fully configured with Sparrow and Python 3 AAMs and clearly marked with two aerial victories. Several sources claim the aircraft has been erroneously marked for years as a double MiG killer. The same sources state this aircraft only has a half kill to its credit, sharing the other half with Baz 832. *O. Zidon Collection*

8 June 1982
F-15C, No. 818
Tamnoon / Octopus
Double Tail Squadron
Maj. Shaul Simon

F-15C-28-MC 80-0125 No. 818—aircraft destroyed: 1 MiG-23; weapon: AIM-7F Sparrow AAM. On 8 June 1982, Capt. Maj. Shaul Simon (Baz 818) and his wingman, Debi Rosenthal (Baz 832), engaged the same SyAAF MiG-23. In the confusion of battle both pilots simultaneously locked on the Flogger and launched an AIM-7F. The evidence is not exactly clear which missile impacted with the MiG first, so the kill is listed as a shared victory.

Baz 832 on static display during an IASF air show. Now assigned to Spearhead Squadron, the aircraft is marked with one and a half SyAAF roundels, adding to the confusion of just how many kills this F-15 and F-15 Baz 818 actually have. In Shlomo Aloni's book *Israeli F-15 Eagle Units in Combat* there is a similar photograph of 818 marked with one and a half kills. *O. Zidon Collection*

8 June 1982
F-15C, No. 832
Ha Shishi Be Yuni /
  The Sixth of June
Double Tail Squadron
Capt. Dedi Rosenthal

F-15C-29-MC 80-0128 No. 832—aircraft destroyed: 1 MiG-23; weapon: AIM-7F Sparrow AAM. It was Capt. Dedi Rosenthal's AIM-7F Sparrow missile that claimed the second half of the 8 June 1982 kill of a SyAAF MiG-23. When the engagement took place Rosenthal was flying on the wing of Maj. Shaul Simon. The pair had separated from their four-ship flight when the kill was made.

Baz No. 832, nicknamed *Ha Shishi Be Yuni* (The Sixth of June), is taxiing after landing. Hardly noticeable on the nose of the aircraft is a half roundel identifying the shared kill of 8 June 1982 with Baz No. 818. *S. Stiller Collection*

9 June 1982
F-15C, No. 684
Ha Raped / The Vampire
Double Tail Squadron
Maj. Ronen Shapira
Maj. Yoram Peled

F-15C-18-MC 76-1516 No. 684—aircraft destroyed: 1 MiG-23, 1 MiG-21; weapon: AIM-7F Sparrow AAM / Python 3 AAM. The MiG-23 was in full afterburner to the east of Maj. Ronen Shapira when he visually acquired and identified the enemy jet. Shapira obtained a radar lock-on, and at approximately 1,500 meters [1,640 yards] fired one of his Sparrow missiles that tracked and impacted with the Syrian MiG. The MiG was seen exploding in a huge fireball.

Maj. Yoram Peled flew No. 684 on the afternoon CAP mission from Tel-Nof Air Base, and like Shapira claimed a kill over a SyAAF MiG-21. Peled was leading a four-ship flight of F-15s when they crossed a mountain ridge and entered Lebanon Valley, becoming engaged with a number of Syrian fighters. In the ensuing air battle the CAP downed a number of Syrian fighters. One MiG-21 was credited to Peled. The Fishbed was shot down with a Python 3 air-to-air missile.

Vampire Baz 684 heavily armed with AIM-7 Sparrows and Python 3 air-to-air missiles tucked under the wings. Having served with the IASF for some time, this aircraft was lost in a mid-air collision on 15 August 1988. Baz 684 was named *Ha Raped* (The Vampire) when the F-15C claimed two MiG kills on 9 June 1982. Why the aircraft is marked with three kill markings is unknown; the third may be a squadron kill. *O. Zidon Collection*

Another Double Tail Squadron Baz with multiple aerial victories is No. 802. The F-15A know by the nickname *Panther* has 4 (3 MiG-23s and 1 MiG-21) confirmed kills and is demonstrating the sheer power of a full afterburner takeoff. *A. Zohar Collection*

9 June 1982
10 June 1982
F-15C, No. 802
Panther
Double Tail Squadron
Lt. Col. Moshe Melnik
Capt. Noam Knaani

F-15C-27-MC 80-0122 No. 802—aircraft destroyed: 3 MiG-23s, 1 MiG-21; weapon: AIM-7F Sparrow AAM / Python 3 AAM. On 9 June 1982, Lt. Col. Moshe Melnik was leading a four-ship CAP when they engaged, fired on, and destroyed four Syrian aircraft. Melnik locked on to a Russian Flogger with a radar guided air-to-air missile, and after firing the weapon it guided to the target and destroyed the MiG upon impact. After the engagement the four F-15s returned to their CAP mission, where the flight encountered a pair of MiG-21s. The SyAAF MiGs were able to launch a number of AAMs at the IASF Baz, but fortunately for the Israeli pilots the Syrian missile failed to hit their targets. Seizing on the opportunity Melnik engaged one of the Fishbeds and launched a Python 3 that tracked true to the target. While engaged Melnik's wingman, Capt. Avi Maor, smoked the second MiG with his 20 mm internal cannon.

Capt. Noam Knaani from Double Tail Squadron was flying Baz 802 the day after Melnik claimed two SyAAF MiGs flying Baz 802. Knaani was on a CAP mission when he engaged, fired on, and destroyed two MiG-23s. Capt. Knaani's weapon of choice was the Python 3 air-to-air missile.

One of only three F-15s of the IASF credited with four aerial victories, Baz 802 is in formation with another F-15. While assigned to Spearhead Squadron in May 1994, 802 was heavily damaged during a landing accident at Tel-Nof Air Base. *Panther* was repaired and continues to fly with the IASF. *O. Zidon Collection*

No. 848, nickname *Nesher* (Eagle), during its arrival at Tel-Nof Air Base. MiG killer 848 appears in a clean condition, suggesting the pilot may have just completed a training sortie. In this post-Lebanon War photograph the Double Tail Squadron frontline fighter is still displaying two Syrian roundels, proclaiming its two kills on 10 June 1982. *O. Zidon Collection*

Baz No. 848 after upgrading, giving the aircraft the ability not only to perform air-to-air missions, but air-to-ground missions. Baz No. 848 has been prepared for an air-to-ground mission configuration with three JADAM bombs, along with a pair of Rafael Python 3s. *O. Zidon Collection*

10 June 1982
F-15C, No. 848
Nesher / Eagle
Double Tail Squadron
Capt. Yoram Hoffman
Capt. Ziv Nadivi

F-15C-29-MC 80-0130 No. 848—aircraft destroyed: 1 MiG-21, 1 Gazelle; weapon: 20 mm cannon / Python 3 AAM. F-15 Baz pilot Capt. Yoram Hoffman of Double Tail Squadron claimed his second aerial victory flying F-15 *Nesher* (Eagle), downing a SyAAF MiG-21 with 20 mm cannon fire. This was one of only two cannon kills during the Lebanon War.

Capt. Ziv Nadivi was credited with the only non-fixed wing kill of the Lebanon War. On 10 June 1982, he was able to gain a position of advantage on a low and slow flying Syrian Gazelle helicopter. Once he had the enemy chopper locked up he launched one Python 3 that tracked to the target. The Gazelle was destroyed in the explosion.

For many years Baz 840 was credited and marked with six aerial victories. It is known the aircraft surely downed four Syrian MiGs during combat service with the IASF. No. 840 is clearly marked with six SyAAF roundels on the fuselage below the canopy. Later research showed the aircraft can only claim four aerial victories. *O. Zidon Collection*

10 June 1982
11 June 1982
19 November 1985
F-15C, No. 840
Commando
Double Tail Squadron
Spearhead Squadron
Lt. Col. Benny Zinker
Lt. Col. Yiftach Shadmi
Maj. Avner Naveh

F-15C-29-MC 80-0129 No. 840—aircraft destroyed: 1 MiG-25, 3 MiG-23s, 1 MiG-21; weapon: Python 3 AAM / 20 mm cannon. Lt. Col. Benny Zinker claimed his first MiG kill as an F-15 pilot on 13 February 1981, when he became the first pilot in history to take out a Russian built MiG-25 Foxbat with the AIM-7F Sparrow missile. He added to his tally on 10 June 1982, when he engaged, fired on, and destroyed a SyAAF MiG-23 with a Python 3.

On 11 June 1982, the Israeli and Syrian governments agreed to a cease-fire. Before the cease-fire took effect, the IASF would claim an additional five SyAAF MiGs. One of the last five kills of the 1982 Lebanon War was by Lt. Col. Yiftach Shadmi from Double Tail Squadron; while on a CAP he destroyed a MiG-21 with 20 mm cannon fire. Of the 33 kills credited to the Baz during the war only two were by gun.

On 19 November 1985, Spearhead Squadron F-15s flown by Maj. Avner Naveh, Yuval Ben Dor, and Ofer Paz were operating with a flight of F-16s when the Syrian Air Force launched a flight of MiG-23s to intercept them. Maj. Avner Naveh had since become CO of Spearhead Squadron when the flight was vectored by ground control to engage the Floggers. The flight initially engaged the Syrians with AIM-7F Sparrow missiles, all of which failed to guide. Switching to the Python 3, Naveh downed two of the MiG-23s, bringing his tally of Baz kills to 6.5.

When Baz 828 claimed its kill on 10 June 1982, Capt. Gil Rapaport and his MiG killer were assigned to Double Tail Squadron. Here No. 828 is in the postwar markings of Spearhead Squadron. Named *Eagle Owl*, No. 828 is in full afterburner taking off. Silhouetted against the blue sky, the sleek lines and brute force of the F-15 are clearly evident. *O. Zidon Collection*

10 June 1982
F-15C, No. 828
O'ach / Eagle Owl
Double Tail Squadron
Capt. Gil Rapaport

F-15C-28-MC 80-0127 No. 828—aircraft destroyed: 1 MiG-23; weapon: Python 3 AAM. During the first days of the Lebanon War, IASF aircraft involved in Operation MIVTZA ARTZA TSHA-ESREH (MOLE CRICKET 19) attacked and destroyed numerous Syrian SAM sites. F-15s from Double Tail Squadron flew CAP for the strike aircraft involved in the suppression of enemy air defenses (SEAD). During one CAP mission, Capt. Gil Rapaport aligned himself behind a SyAAF MiG-21 and once in range launched a Python 3 that tracked directly to the MiG and exploded on impact.

On 10 June 1982, when Schwartz and Shapira claimed their MiG-21 Fishbed, the tail number of the aircraft was 708. Most if not all of the F-15s with the prefix digit "7" were replaced with a "4." Here Baz 408 is still assigned to Double Tail Squadron and still decorated with the kill marking crediting Schwartz and Shapira with their MiG-21 kill. *O. Zidon Collection*

Baz No. 408 (*Chariot of Fire*) has undergone a transformation from strictly an air superiority fighter to a multi-role fighter, clearly indicating 408 can be configured with JADAM weapons for an air-to-ground mission. *O. Zidon Collection*

10 June 1982
F-15B, No. 408
Merkevet Esh /
Chariot of Fire
Double Tail Squadron
Capt. Shaul Schwartz
Uzi Shapira

F-15B-16-MC 76-1525 No. 408—aircraft destroyed: 1 MiG-21; weapon: Python 3 AAM. Capt. Shaul Schwartz was the pilot of Baz 708 (changed to 408) when he claimed his second MiG kill of the war. Schwartz and his navigator, Uzi Shapira, were flying as part of CAP formation over the Lebanon Valley when they engaged and destroyed a MiG-21 with a Python 3.

Triple MiG killer Baz 979 touches down after completing its mission. In the markings of Spearhead Squadron, F-15 *Wings Wave* still proudly displays three kill markings from the Lebanon War. Some sources claim that a high 10 to 12 G turn put on the airframe of 979 by Feldsho and Lipsitz during their double kill on 24 June 1982 left the airframe twisted and it remains so to this day. *O. Zidon Collection*

Battle tested Baz No. 979, with three confirmed aerial victories to its credit during 1982, stands on alert with Spearhead Squadron. The weapons configuration includes highly effective Rafael Popeye guided munitions, a fuel tank under the port side wing, and three highly effective Python 3 AAMs. *O. Zidon Collection*

10 June 1982

24 June 1982

F-15D, No. 979

Mashak Knafaim /
 Wings Wave

Double Tail Squadron

Spearhead Squadron

Maj. Yoram Peled

Maj. Zvi Lipsitz

Maj. Zvi Lipsitz

F-15D-28-MC 80-0136 No. 979—aircraft destroyed: 1 MiG-21, 2 MiG-23s; weapon: Python 3 AAM. Baz 979 was the last of the Peace Fox III F-15Ds sent to the IASF. Bearing the nickname *Wings Wave*, No. 979 was flown by Maj. Yoram Peled and Maj. Zvi Lipsitz on 10 June 1982, when they downed a SyAAF MiG-21 by way of a Python 3. Of the thirty-three aerial victories credited to the F-15 during the Lebanon War, nineteen were accomplished with the Israeli produced Python 3. Approximately two weeks later Maj. Zvi Lipsitz was again in the back seat of No. 979 when he and Maj. Yoel Feldsho downed two MiG-23s.

The cease-fire of 11 June 1982 did not end the fighting in Lebanon; in fact, it continued well into August 1982. IASF continued air operations, attacking targets throughout Lebanon pretty much unopposed by the Syrian Air Force.

Syria did send MiG-23s against the IASF on 24 June 1982. Maj. Yoel Feldsho and his navigator, Maj. Zvi Lipsitz, were leading a CAP flight (call sign Hot) when they were vectored by ground control to intercept the MiGs over Baalbeck. Feldsho acquired the MiGs over Rayak, in enemy controlled territory. At approximately eight hundred meters (875 yards) he launched a Python that destroyed the first of the two MiGs.

Shortly after engaging and downing the first Flogger Hot lead engaged the second enemy MiG. Pulling into a 10–12 G turn, Feldsho and Lipsitz were able to obtain an advantageous position to fire a second Python 3 that also found its mark, destroying the second SyAAF MiG.

No. 455 safely landing in the markings of Double Tail Squadron. Painted on the fuselage under the cockpit are two kill markings. This aircraft was only credited with one MiG kill during the Lebanon War. The second roundel identifies this aircraft as being one of the F-15s that participated in Operation WOODEN LEG. *O. Zidon Collection*

10 June 1982
F-15D, No. 455
Roach Partzim /
**   Stormy Wind**
Double Tail Squadron
Maj. Mickey Lev

F-15D-27-MC 80-0132 No. 455—aircraft destroyed: 1 MiG-21; weapon: Python 3 AAM. On 10 June 1982, Maj. Mickey Lev was flying in a four-ship CAP when he tangled with a SyAAF Fishbed (MiG-21) over the Lebanon Valley. The IASF pilot was able to visually identify the enemy aircraft. The enemy aircraft was well within range of the Python 3 and once a good tone was established he fired the weapon. The missile was seen guiding to the target and detonating, destroying the MiG. Lev failed to pull off the target quick enough and as a result flew through the debris field of the exploding MiG, causing damage. The Baz remained flyable and he made it home safely.

When Lev flew his MiG kill mission the tail number of the aircraft was No. 955. Upon transfer to Double Tail Squadron the prefix was changed to a "4." Even though this aircraft is a two-seat "D" model, Lev was alone in the aircraft on 10 June.

Baz 667 in a hardened shelter while assigned to Double Tail Squadron. The Hebrew printing on the nose is the aircraft's nickname, which in English translates to Cyclone. The roundel painted on the nose stands in testament to the 10 June 1982 MiG-21 kill of Lt. Col. Yiftach Shadmi. *O. Zidon Collection*

10 June 1982
F-15A, No. 667
Tzikion / Cyclone
Double Tail Squadron
Lt. Col. Yiftach Shadmi

F-15A-17-MC 76-1509 No. 667—aircraft destroyed: 1 MiG-21; weapon: Python 3 AAM. Another Double Tail Squadron kill from 10 June 1982 was by Lt. Col. Yiftach Shadmi; at the time of his MiG encounter he was flying on the wing of Maj. Yoram Peled and Maj. Zvi Lipsitz when each of them shot down a Syrian MiG-23. The Syrian Arab Air Force not only scrambled the two Floggers on the tenth, but also a pair of MiG-21s. While Peled and Lipsitz were heavily engaged with the flight of MiG-23s, Shadmi went after one of the MiG-21s, which he easily dispatched with a Python 3.

Baz 678 stands on a five minute alert secured in a hardened shelter at the home of Double Tail Squadron, Tel Nof Air Base. If forced to scramble, this F-15 is configured with the new Python 4 air-to-air missile and will surely present a formidable adversary for any intruder. *O. Zidon Collection*

11 June 1982
F-15A, No. 678
Ha Yo'reh / The Shooter
Double Tail Squadron
Maj. Yoram Peled

F-15A-17-MC 76-1514 (678)—aircraft destroyed: 2 MiG-23s; weapon: AIM-7F Sparrow AAM. Maj. Yoram Peled was flying lead in Adulthood flight on a CAP when SyAAF aircraft were discovered operating over Rayak. Being vectored toward the formation of enemy aircraft, Adulthood flight acquired the aircraft and positively identified them as MiG-23s.

Peled was able to maneuver to within a few miles of the trailing MiG and launch a radar guided missile in look-down shoot-down mode. The missile tracked beautifully and quickly impacted with the aft section of the Flogger. Without hesitation Peled reacquired the lead MiG and readied a second Sparrow for launch. Once locked on the missile was fired, and like the first missile tracked to the MiG. The resulting impact and explosion destroyed the lead enemy MiG.

F-15C No. 821, flown by Capt. Shaul Schwartz on his 31 August 1982 mission, is seen in April 1982 being turned over to aircraft maintainers at Tel-Nof Air Base. Baz 821 wears the Hebrew name *Peres* (English translation Lammergeyer, meaning large old world vulture, which in flight resembles a huge falcon). This aircraft was lost in a training accident on 10 February 1991, in which pilot Israel Ornan was killed. *A. Dor Collection*

31 August 1982
F-15C, No. 821
Peres / Lammergeyer
Spearhead Squadron
Capt. Shaul Schwartz

F-15C-27-MC 80-0126 No. 821—aircraft destroyed: 1 MiG-25; weapon: AIM-7F Sparrow AAM. Russian piloted MiG-25RB Foxbats were overflying Lebanon on photo reconnaissance missions virtually untouched by IASF aircraft. The Israelis devised a plan to ambush the MiG-25s (code name Nestling) on their next reconnaissance flight.

On 31 August 1982, the Israelis set the ambush in motion when they discovered a high flying, fast moving Nestling over Beirut. The Israelis had positioned a Hawk missile battery to engage the MiG-25 and once locked on it fired two Hawk surface-to-air missiles. The missiles exploded in close proximity to the fast moving Foxbat. The explosion damaged the MiG-25; trailing black smoke, it was picked up by an IASF F-15 Baz. Capt. Shaul Schwartz locked on the descending MiG with an AIM-7F Sparrow missile and quickly terminated the MIG.

Official records credit Schwartz and the Hawk missile battery with a shared kill for the 31 August 1982 shoot-down of the MiG-25RB Foxbat.

CHAPTER 6
Operation WOODEN LEG

MIVTZA REGAL ETZ

When Israel picked the F-15 Eagle over the F-14 Tomcat in head-to-head evaluation in the mid-'70s, they were looking for more than a one-dimensional aircraft. The Israeli team was not only evaluating air-to-air capabilities, but if the design of the Eagle offered the flexibility to be an all-weather strike fighter. Sometime in the 1980s work was conducted to modify F-15s to perform long-range precision strike missions. In 1985, the Israeli Baz shocked the world when they carried out the longest air strike in the history of the Israeli Air Force.

On 25 September 1985, a group of Palestine Liberation Organization (PLO) terrorists killed three unarmed Israeli civilians who were holidaying on their yacht off Larnaca, Cyprus. Credit for this cowardly act was claimed by Force 17, a section within the PLO.

In response to a recent rocket attack into a settlement in northern Israel and the unprovoked murder of the three Israeli civilians, the Israeli government voted to approve a retaliatory air strike against the PLO.

On 1 October 1985, the IASF launched Operation MIVTZA REGEL ETZ (WOODEN LEG) from Tel Nof Air Base against POL headquarters in Hammam al-Shatt, Tunisia, about twelve miles from the capital, Tunis. The mission would prove to be the longest air strike the IASF had undertaken since Entebbe in 1976, and it is believed the mission was the first time the F-15 Baz was used as a strike fighter. The strike aircraft would have to fly more than 1,280 miles over open water. To accomplish the long range mission two modified Boeing 707 tankers from Desert Giant squadron would meet the strike aircraft mid-flight over the Mediterranean Sea. Having rendezvoused with the two Boeing 707 tankers and completed the in-flight refueling phase, the two flights of Baz would continue on their designed flight profile, avoiding deployments in the Mediterranean. The operational aspects of the mission would be directed and controlled by highly experienced command personnel flying in a specially equipped Boeing 707 airborne command post.

The aircraft selected by the IASF to deliver the blow were the F-15B/D Baz of Spearhead Squadron. Having proven itself in the Lebanon War as an interceptor, the F-15 would now prove itself as an effective bomber. It has long been accepted that the Zora Ha'Avir Ve'Halalal were the first to deploy the F-15 Baz in the strike aircraft role. The aircraft and pilots for WOODEN LEG were all GBU-15 weapons qualified for the mission. The actual air strike on the target was to be carried out by two strike flights of F-15s armed with unpowered GBU-15 electro-optical glide weapons.

The first six F-15s to hit the seaside PLO headquarters were assigned to deliver GBU-15s on their designated targets. The GBU-15 is a highly maneuverable weapon and has an optimal, low-to-medium altitude delivery capability with pinpoint accuracy. The last two F-15s over the target were armed with unguided general purpose (GP) Mk 82 500 lb. bombs.

The air strike, which was accomplished in six minutes, destroyed almost the entire PLO complex, including the PLO chairman's bureau and the headhunters of Force 17. Between sixty and a hundred terrorists were killed and another seventy were wounded.

Aftermath of MIVTZA REGAL ETZ

Without missing a beat, the worldwide condemnation of Israel's attack against Yasser Arafat's PLO was swift and unrelenting. From the Middle East to the United Nations (UN), and even Israel's strongest ally, the United States, expressed strong objections to Operation WOODEN LEG.

The burning question for enemies of Israel in the Middle East and their sponsors in the Kremlin was how did Israel carry out the longest range attack in its history? How were they able to avoid detection from Egyptian and Libyan radar units, and even US Navy ships deployed in the Mediterranean?

The answers to these questions are like those raised during Operation JONATHAN, the rescue mission in Entebbe, Uganda (1976); and Operation OPERA (1981), the air strike against the Osirak nuclear reactor ten miles southeast of Baghdad, Iraq.

The enduring legacy within the IASF over its enemies is not necessarily its overwhelming superiority in weapons technology, nor its enemies being technically inept. It is the personal qualities of the IASF's men and women, for humans will always be the final power in war.

The men and women of the IASF had the foresight to realize the full potential of the Baz dual role capabilities when the F-15 was chosen. Once integrated into the IASF, inventory plans to upgrade the capabilities of the F-15 were undertaken. Many still are of the opinion that the F-15s that carried out the air strike against PLO headquarters in Tunis were American manufactured F-15E Strike Eagles.

The strike package that carried out Operation WOODEN LEG was F-15C/Ds modified during the summer of 1985, well before the introduction of the F-15E in April 1988. IASF modifications gave the F-15s the capability of performing long range missions with the addition of conformal fuel tanks (CFT). Improvements also included advanced avionics and radar, weapons control, and electronic warfare systems.

The modifications made to the F-15C/D models by Israel enhanced the aircraft's ability to carry out long-range, high-speed dual role missions and made Operation WOODEN LEG possible. The IASF continues to modify its Baz and Netz. Continued upgrades have produced two of the world's premier dual role high-speed interdiction aircraft: the F-15I Ra'am (Thunder) and F-16I Sufa (Storm) are fitted with custom designed and manufactured Israeli electronics. The Ra'am and Sufa have also been designed to carry American and Israeli weapons for air-to-air and air-to-ground missions.

Many important aspects of Operation WOODEN LEG are still classified. The identities of the F-15 Baz listed herein are based on the best information available.

F-15 Baz of Operation Mivtza Regal Etz (WOODEN LEG)

| 1 October 1985 |
| F-15D, No. 280 |
| Yad Ha Nefetz / |
| Shutter Hand |
| Spearhead Squadron |
| Classified |
| Classified |

F-15D-35-MC 83-0064 No. 280—target PLO headquarters; weapon: GBU-15 electro-optical glide bombs. The two-seat F-15D Baz 280 was one of the handpicked aircraft participating in the Tunis Raid. Tail No. 280 was armed with GBU-15 electro-optical glide bombs. The attacking IASF jets caught the PLO terrorists totally off guard and were able to place their weapons on target with great accuracy.

Baz 280 lifting off from Tel-Nof Air Base in the tail markings of Double Tail Squadron. Painted on the fuselage by the nickname of the aircraft is a special emblem (roundel with a GBU-15 bomb) denoting the 1 October 1985 Tunis Raid. Tail No. 280 is one of the strike aircraft credited with a direct hit on its target with the GBU-15. *O. Zidon Collection*

The hostile landscape in the background gives the impression IASF F-15 Tail No. 450 is taking off from another planet. This particular Baz was unable to deliver its GUB-15s on target during Operation WOODEN LEG. The operation proved the IASF surely possessed the capability of reaching out to attack the PLO and other terrorist organizations. *O. Zidon Collection*

1 October 1985
F-15D, No. 450
Cherev Pipiyot /
**   Two Edge Sword**
Spearhead Squadron
Classified
Classified

F-15D-27-MC 80-0131 No. 450—target PLO headquarters; weapon: GBU-15 electro-optical glide bombs. During WOODEN LEG, Baz No. 450 was one of six strike aircraft armed with GBU-15s used to destroy the PLO complex. Unfortunately, 450 returned six hours later, having failed to deploy its weapons. Baz No. 450 was unable to deliver ordnance on the target when the aircraft experienced a technical malfunction with its bomb delivery system.

Double Tail Squadron F-15D No. 455 climbs into a beautiful blue sky. The aircraft is marked with two roundels: one commemorating the Baz aerial victory during the Lebanon War, and the second its participation in Operation WOODEN LEG. *A. Zohar Collection*

1 October 1985
F-15D, No. 455
Roach Partzim /
   Stormy Wind
Spearhead Squadron
Classified

F-15D-27-MC 80-0132 No. 455—target PLO headquarters; weapon: GBU-15 electro-optical glide bomb. When IASF aircraft flew Operation WOODEN LEG, all national and unit markings were removed. No. 455 was another of the bomb-laden F-15s credited with direct hits on the PLO complex.

Touch down! While Baz 970 returns safely home another F-15 is taking off. Because of the present state of the Middle East, IASF aircraft are continually flying training or real world combat missions. The IASF maintains aircraft on a constant state of alert to respond to any aggressive act toward Israel. During the real world mission of 1 October 1985, Tail No. 970 flew on the wing of the leader of WOODEN LEG. *O. Zidon Collection*

1 October 1985
F-15D, No. 970
Ayelet Hashachar /
    Morning Star
Spearhead Squadron
Classified
Classified

F-15D-28-MC 80-0135 No. 970—target PLO headquarters; weapon: GBU-15 electro-optical glide bomb. The attack on 1 October 1985 against the PLO headquarters in Tunis clearly demonstrated the long-range capabilities of IASF F-15s. This F-15D was one of the attackers of the PLO complex able to place its GBU-15 glide bombs directly on target during WOODEN LEG. Throughout the mission the IASF aircraft went unchallenged by Tunisian and Syrian Air Forces. The attack was such a surprise the IASF aircraft were not even challenged by anti-aircraft defenses within the complex.

Iconic Baz No. 957 (Sky Blazer), with four and a half aerial victories to its credit, has been involved in numerous combat actions besides Operation MIVTZA REGAL ETZ. It is seen arriving in the Czech Republic on 22 September 2011. *R. Kolek Collection*

1 October 1985
F-15D, No. 957
Mrkia Shchakim /
   Sky Blazer
Spearhead Squadron
Classified
Classified

F-15D-28-MC 80-0133 No. 957—target PLO headquarters; weapon: GBU-15 electro-optical glide bomb. The Tunis Raid (Operation MIVTZA REGAL ETZ) proved unequivocally that Israel possessed the capability to strike targets far from home. Baz 957 was tasked to deliver GBU-15 electro-optical glide bombs on the main complex of PLO headquarters in Tunis on 1 October 1985.

Utilizing brute force, tail No. 530 is captured in full afterburner. Taken in August 2005, Tail No. 530 was taking part in the first full-scale Flying Dragon Squadron exercise in the skies over Ovda. *O. Zidon Collection*

1 October 1985
F-15C, No. 530
Chetz / Arrow
Spearhead Squadron
Classified

F-15C-36-MC 83-0057 No. 530—target PLO headquarters; weapon: General Purpose free fall 500 lb. iron bombs. Baz No. 530 was one of two single-seat F-15Ds that flew the historic WOODEN LEG operation. The two "D" models were the seventh and eight aircraft over the PLO complex in Tunis. Both F-15s released their six 500 lb. Mk-82 bombs carried on the center line of the aircraft.

1 October 1985
F-15C, No. 840
Commando
Spearhead Squadron
Classified
Classified

F-15C-29-MC 80-0129 No. 840—target PLO headquarters; weapon: General Purpose free fall 500 lb. bombs. Baz No. 840 was one of the aircraft configured with six Mk-82 bombs carried on the centerline mutable ejection racks. It is not known who piloted this Baz during the operation. Seven of the pilots were already credited with MiG kills, and the eighth pilot would claim his first MiG kill a month after the raid. Prior to the operation Baz 840, like the pilots, was also a confirmed MiG killer: 1 MiG-25, 3 MiG-23s, and 1 MiG-21.

Baz 840 taking fuel from an American tanker. The purpose and location is unknown. *A. Dorr Collection*

F-15I No. 238 is configured for an air-to-ground mission armed with the highly effective AGM-142 Have Nap (Popeye) cruise missile. The Have Nap is a homegrown weapon system designed and built by Rafael Advanced Defense System/Lockheed Martin; it can deliver its 750 lb. blast fragmentation or 800 lb. penetrator warheads over forty-eight miles with an amazing degree of accuracy. *O. Zidon Collection.*

F-15I Ra'am – Thunder
No. 69 Squadron, Ha' Patishim (Hammers)

During Operation DESERT STORM, Iraq managed to launch 40-plus surface-to-surface Al-Hussein (Soviet R-17E SCUD B) missiles into Israel. As a result of the successful launch against Israel, military and political leadership realized the need for a new weapon system. The aircraft would have to possess the ability to strike at Israel's major present day threat, Iran. The weapon system decided on was the American F-15E Strike Eagle. Like most aircraft in IASF inventory, the American version would be specially designed and modified to meet the needs of the IASF.

The F-15I Ra'am (Thunder) is a true masterpiece from a purely technological standpoint. The dual role fighter has the ability to combine long-range interdiction, day or night, in all weather conditions against high value targets. The Ra'am is superbly air-to-air capable at speeds of Mach 2.5 and its air-to-air weapons. The F-15I (I for Israel) externally looks similar to the United States Air Force F-15E Strike Eagle, but for the most part that is where the similarities end. The F-15I Ra'am, unlike the American F-15E, is painted in a three-tone desert camouflage brown-green-gray paint. Prominently painted and displayed on the tail of the Ra'am is a large head of an eagle.

The capabilities of No. 69 Ha'Patishim Squadron are a closely guarded secret. What little is known indicates the F-15I is packed with the most modern and sophisticated electronic countermeasure equipment. Most of the cutting edge systems are Israeli designed and manufactured to deal foremost with the Iranian threat.

The F-15I incorporates new and unique weapons that enhance its ability to deliver a tremendous payload on targets at a very low altitude. Within six months of becoming operational with No. 69 Squadron the Ra'am carried out its first air-to-ground combat mission in southern Lebanon. On 11 June 1999, a pair of F-15Is attacked suspected Hezbollah terrorist targets on Soujud Ridge with precision guided munitions. Shortly thereafter they were involved in a nighttime operation to destroy two bridges over the Litany and Awali Rivers.

F-15Is operating with Hammer Squadron are without a doubt the premier multi-purpose fighter of the Zroa Ha' Avir Ve' Halalal. F-15I Thunder No. 252 is armed with a unique asymmetric weapons load. F-15Is of Hammer Squadron stand on alert fully armed and prepared to respond to any aggressive act toward Israel. *O. Zidon Collection*

CHAPTER 7

ROYAL SAUDI AIR FORCE
F-15 AERIAL VICTORIES

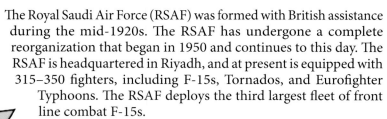

Royal Saudi AF coat of arms

The Royal Saudi Air Force (RSAF) was formed with British assistance during the mid-1920s. The RSAF has undergone a complete reorganization that began in 1950 and continues to this day. The RSAF is headquartered in Riyadh, and at present is equipped with 315–350 fighters, including F-15s, Tornados, and Eurofighter Typhoons. The RSAF deploys the third largest fleet of front line combat F-15s.

Saudi Arabia may very well be the best-equipped military in the Gulf region and maintains a constant state of readiness to deal with the perceived threat from Iran. Since June 1984, the RSAF's F-15 Eagles have bloodied their talons in air-to-air combat on at least two occasions.

Eagle and Phantom II Battle over the Persian Gulf

5 June 1984
F-15D, No. 1301, (502)
13th Squadron, Royal Saudi Air Force
Unknown

F-15D-30-MC 80-0083 No. 1301—aircraft destroyed: 1 (2?) F-4E Phantom II; weapon: AIM-7 Sparrow air-to-air missile. Royal Saudi Air Force F-15D No. 1301 was originally received from the United States under Operation PEACE SUN as No. 502. At some point the Eagle was renumbered by the RSAF as No. 1301.

This computer generated image depicts the events of 5 June 1984, when two Saudi Air Force F-15s from 13th Squadron intercepted a pair of Iranian F-4Es belonging to No. 61 Battalion of IRIAF that intruded into Saudi air space. *Digital Artwork by Najam Khan, Pakistan*

5 June 1984

On the fifteenth of Khurdad 1363 (Persian Calendar), during the Iran-Iraq War, an aerial engagement took place between Iranian F-4E Phantom IIs and Saudi Arabian F-15 Eagles that ended with the destruction of at least one or possibly two of the Iranian F-4E Phantom IIs.

Thirty-three years later, the details of 5 June 1984 are still quite obscure about the Eagle vs. Phantom II battle over the Persian Gulf. It has been difficult at best to accurately confirm the details surrounding the air battle. Official sources, along with domestic and external sources, indicate the air battle indeed took place.

News agencies reported from the United States that Airborne Early Warning and Control System (AWACS) aircraft identified the Iranian F-4E Phantom IIs and determined the Phantoms were operating in Saudi Arabia's airspace. The two F-4Es of Battalion 61 from Bushehr Air Base, 6th Tactical Air Base, were deployed.

The two Iranian Air Force (IAF) Phantoms were being vectored to Lavan Island, off the coast of Saudi Arabia.

IAF surveillance aircraft (P-3F Orion) operating in the area had targeted a large oil tanker heading to Iraq for destruction. While the two Phantoms were being vectored toward the tanker they were discovered by an AWACS (E-3A) aircraft operating over the Persian Gulf.

Coincidently, two Saudi Air Force F-15 Eagles (an F-15C and F-15D) belonging to No. 6 Squadron were refueling from an American KC-10 tanker. The E-3A ordered the RASF F-15s to immediately cease refueling and intercept the IAF Phantoms

The E-3A AWACS played a crucial role directing Saudi F-15s on 5 June 1984, during the interception of Iranian Air Force F-4E Phantoms that entered Saudi airspace. The role of the E-3A is to carry out airborne surveillance and command and control. The E-3A can track and direct air and sea targets simultaneously. *USAF photograph*

The Iranian Phantoms were intercepted south of Al-Jubayl naval base by Saudi F-15s. The Eagles of the RSAF engaged the Phantoms in a head-on attack. It has been reported each F-15 launched an air-to-air Sparrow AIM-7 missile at the closing Phantoms. One of the Iranian F-4Es exploded in an instant when struck by an AIM-7, while the second Phantom sustained severe damage.

The aircrew of the destroyed Iranian aircraft have been identified as Lt. Col. Humayum Hekmati and Capt. Sayed Serwas Karimi. The severely damaged Phantom is reported to have landed on the Kish Island in Iran.

American Involvement
The United States and Saudi governments have never fully explained the air battle of 5 June 1984. Domestic sources in Iran and external sources agree that two RSAF F-15s did shoot down one Iranian F-4E and severely damaged a second one. The Iranians claim the attack of 5 June was under the command of an American Air Force F-15 instructor pilot, Capt. Bill Tippin. Capt. Tippin's involvement in the air battle has never been fully explained by the USAF, nor the Saudi Air Force. Internal sources in Iran claim Tippin was acting as the Weapons System Operator (WSO) in the Saudi F-15D. Other sources claim he was the pilot of the aircraft and not the WSO.

Maj. General Spencer M. "SAM" Armstrong, USAF (Ret.)
US Military Training Mission
Royal Saudi Air Force
July 1983 to July 1985

Maj. Gen. Spencer M. "SAM" Armstrong is a highly decorated United States Air Force command pilot with over 4,500 flying hours. During his tour in Southeast Asia, Gen. Armstrong was assigned to the 34th Tactical Fighter Squadron (TFS), Korat RTAFB, Thailand. While assigned to the 34th TFS, the general accumulated 283 additional combat hours in the F-105 while flying 100 missions over North Vietnam against the most heavily defended targets (Paul Doumer Bridge, Dragon's Jaw Bridge, Canal des Rapides Railroad Bridge, and the Northeast Rail Line and others).

From July 1983 to July 1985, Gen. Armstrong was commander of the US Military Training Mission to the Royal Saudi Air Force. It is during this time the air engagement between Saudi F-15 Eagles and Iranian F-4E Phantoms took place.

When the general was asked about the involvement of USAF pilots he was quick to respond. "In short, there were no USAF pilots involved except in reviewing the film for the RSAF." Gen. Armstrong further stated he knew the names of the USAF F-15 pilots in his command and could not recall a Capt. Bill Tippin.

The following narrative regarding the events of 5 June 1984 is a verbatim account of the incident as presented by Gen. Armstrong to me:

The war between Iran and Iraq was really hot during my two years. Shortly after I got there, the Iranians sunk an Iraqi oil tanker in the Gulf and the Iraqis struck back with their French-made Exocet air-to-surface missiles—the "tanker war" was well underway. The Iranians did not have us to maintain their aircraft anymore so their equipment was in poor shape. The Iraqis soon had the advantage in this war on the Gulf. The Saudis were concerned the Iranians might go after the oil facilities or the desalination plant on the Gulf since the Saudis were assisting the Iraqis. They wanted to maintain an F-15 Combat Air Patrol [CAP], but needed in-flight refueling. We obliged by sending two KC-10 tankers over and the 24-hour CAP was begun.

Beth [Mrs. Armstrong] and I were having lunch at the Mission Inn in Dhahran when the chief of the Dhahran advisory detachment came hurrying over. He took me aside and said they had reason to believe there had been a shoot-down over the Gulf. Together we hurried down to the tactical operation center [TOC], where US personnel manned surveillance radar. He told me on the way it appeared two F-15s had shot down one or two Iranian F-4s. I found Col. [Prince] Turki standing by a radar display, talking to some RSAF F-5s. Iranian helicopters were on the Saudi side of the Gulf, apparently looking for survivors. The Saudis got a lot of their intelligence from people on the oil platforms out in the gulf, and one of them reported the helicopter appeared to have missiles. I was pretty sure they were mistaking the skid on the helicopter for missiles, because these were helicopters we had sold to them years earlier. Turki looked at me and asked if I thought we should order the F-5s to shoot down the helicopter. Trigger authority had been delegated to Turki, although he had never had to use it. I shook my head and Turki ordered the F-5s to merely shoo the helicopter away.

When our F-15 pilots had a chance to review the tapes some interesting facts came out. Two Iranian F-14s were headed directly for Dhahran from Busheir while two F-4s had come around the north end of the Gulf and were heading down the Saudi side at low level. The Saudi controller aboard a US AWACS ordered Blue Flight to intercept the F-4s and ordered Yellow Flight—just taking off from Dhahran—to intercept the F-4s. The RSAF major leading Yellow Flight quickly sized up the geometry and ordered Blue Flight to take on the F-4s. The F-14s were merely a feint, as they turned around and went home at the middle of the Gulf.

The two RSAF lieutenants turned hard left and descended for a head-on pass. The closure speed was about 1,200 mph. The F-15 wingman fired at maximum range for a radar missile and the leader must have had a case of "buck fever," since he forgot to jettison his drop tanks and fired a missile at minimum range of effectiveness. They observed two explosions, but they could not tell if the missiles hit the F-4s or merely impacted the Gulf. Since radar contact was lost for both F-4s it was reckoned both F-15s achieved kills. The water was shallow where the plane[s] went down, but very murky conditions prevented the discovery of the wreckage. They did find a seat cushion from an F-4. Each RSAF pilot was presented with a Mercedes 500 SEL as a token of appreciation from the king. Later at Taif, Prince Sultan asked me if they shot down one or two aircraft. I replied that it was one for sure and probably both. He replied they were claiming only one since they did not want to necessarily upset the Iranians anymore than they had to.

Royal Saudi Air Force F-15C No. 1308 is credited with the destruction of 2 Iraqi Mirage F-1EQs during the Gulf War and participated in Anatolian Eagle 2013-2. Anatolian Eagle is a two week long, realistic exercise held in central Turkey. The Saudi F-15s were deployed during the exercise in the air-to-air role. F-15C No. 1308 is executing a maximum performance takeoff. *K. Daws Collection*

24 January 1991
F-15C, No. 1308, (509)
13th Squadron, Royal
**   Saudi Air Force**
Capt. Ayedh al-Shamrani

F-15C-29-MC 80-0068 No. 1308—aircraft destroyed: 2 Mirage F-1EQs; weapon: 2 AIM-9P Sidewinder air-to-air missiles. Royal Saudi Air Force F-15C No. 1308 was originally received from the United States under Operation PEACE SUN as No. 509. At some point the Eagle was renumbered by the RSAF as No. 1308.

On 2 August 1990, the largest military power in the Middle East (Iraq) invaded the tiny country of Kuwait and began criminal occupation of the Arab state. A coalition of thirty-four nations led by President George H. W. Bush (code name DESERT SHIELD) was formed in response to Iraq's invasion and annexation of Kuwait.

On 16 January 1991, after Iraq failed to comply with United Nations mandates, the coalition unleashed Operation DESERT STORM to expel Iraqi troops from Kuwait.

On 24 January 1991, during the height of the air campaign, Capt. Ayedh al-Shamrani—a thirty-year-old RSAF F-15 pilot from 13th Squadron—was directed by an E-3A AWACS control aircraft to intercept a flight of Iraqi aircraft.

Capt. al-Shamrani's four-ship flight located the French-built Iraqi Mirage F-1s streaking low, heading south along the Saudi coast. The Iraqi aircraft appeared to be heading for British warships operating in the Gulf. When intercepted by the Saudi F-15s, the Iraqi Mirage F-1s were configured with Exocert anti-ship missiles and bombs.

Capt. al-Shamrani positively identified the targeted aircraft as Iraqi. He immediately peeled off and closed to within 3,000 feet of the Iraqi fighters. He armed an AIM-9 Sidewinder and upon establishing a good tone, indicating the missile was locked on to the target, he launched the missile and without hesitation engaged a second Mirage. Within minutes two Iraqi Mirage fighters were destroyed. A third Mirage managed to escape after launching an Exocert that fell harmlessly into the sea.

After the engagement the Saudi pilot stated during a media interview: "They started breaking in front of me, but it was too late. It was my day."

Combat tested Eagle No. 1308 is airborne to engage in a simulated air combat mission during Anatolian Eagle. The two-week exercise is structured along the lines of USAF's Red Flag, the Canadian Maple Flag, and the Dutch Frisian Flag exercises. *K. Daws Collection*

CHAPTER 8
Iraq Invasion of Kuwait and Operation DESERT STORM

USAF coat of arms

2 August 1990–28 February 1991

After the eight year (1980–1988) Iran-Iraq War, Iraq was experiencing increasing political and economic isolation. Iraq had accumulated a staggering war debt of over $500 billion (US dollars). Iraq's war debt also accrued more than $130 billion of international debt. Part of the international debt ($65 billion) was owed to Kuwait. Kuwait had refused to forgive the debt when requested by Iraq to do so. Along with her war debt, Iraqi President Saddam Hussein accused Kuwait of stealing oil from the Iraqi Rumaila oil fields near the board of both countries. The war debt and allegation of Kuwait stealing oil may have been a precursor to the events that followed early in August 1990.

The truth may lie more in Iraq's territorial and hegemonic claim that Kuwait and its important sea coast were part of Iraq. Iraq, having limited access to the Gulf, would benefit greatly from the acquisition of Kuwait Bay, a natural deep water harbor.

In early August 1990, Saddam Hussein ordered the invasion and annexation of neighboring Emirate of Kuwait. The conflict erupted between Iraq and Kuwait on 2 August 1990, when elements of the elite Republican Guard crossed into Kuwait, and in a matter of hours began to occupy the capital, Kuwait City. Within two days Saddam Hussein declared Kuwait was now the nineteenth province of Iraq.

The World Response to the Iraqi Invasion

Saddam Hussein totally underestimated the world's response to his invasion of Kuwait. On 3 August 1990, the United Nations Security Council met in an emergency session and expressed international condemnation of Iraq's invasion of Kuwait. The UN Security Council passed Resolution 660, demanding complete withdrawal of Iraqi troops from Kuwait. The resolution further granted the right "to use all necessary means to make them comply."

Fearing Iraq was preparing to invade Saudi Arabia, President George W. H. Bush ordered combat aircraft (F-15s) from the 1st Tactical Fighter Wing, Langley AFB, Virginia, to immediately deploy to Saudi Arabia. On 7 August 1990, the F-15C/Ds from Langley arrived at Dhahran AFB, Saudi Arab.

In response to Iraq's invasion of Kuwait, the major powers of the world assembled a coalition. Led by the United States, Britain, France, Canada, and Italy, the coalition was joined by many Middle Eastern countries: Saudi Arabia and Egypt were joined by Syria, the United Arab Emirates, Oman, and Qatar.

Under Operation DESERT SHIELD, the coalition began to assemble the largest military force since WWII. It was clearly understood the coalition would be facing the IAF, at the time the fourth largest air force in the world. The IAF was built around over 500 Soviet-built MiG-21s, MiG-23s, MiG-25s, and MiG-29s, as well as French-built Mirage F-1s.

Under the command of USAF Lt. Gen. Chuck Horner, the coalition assembled an aerial strike force of over 2,250 combat aircraft. Over 1,800 of the aircraft were USAF and Navy assets.

The Great Duel, "The Mother of All Battles Has Begun…"
During Operation DESERT STORM, USAF F-15 Eagles claimed the vast majority (85%) of aerial combat victories over the IAF. Thirty-three out of 35 fixed-wing kills were obtained by Eagles. The Eagles were able to achieve supremacy through a mixture of unprecedented maneuverability and acceleration. With a substantial portion of the IAF destroyed, inactive, or fleeing, the threat to coalition aircraft was severely reduced.

To date, the F-15s in service with the ISAF, USAF, and RSAF have maintained a perfect air-to-air combat record of 101 victories without a single defeat.

When Eagles Fly—MiGs Die
Operation DESERT STORM Aerial Victories

The ground crew of F-15C No. 85-0125 stands by, waiting for the pilot to start his preflight checklist prior to launching the aircraft on a training mission at Eglin AFB, home of the 33rd Tactical Fighter Wing. Seven years after the Gulf War, F-15C 85-0125 still wears the star identifying its MiG-29 kill of 17 January 1991. This F-15 is now on display in a roadside park in De Barry, Florida. *P. Martin Collection*

17 January 1991
F-15C, No. 85-0125
58th TFS, 33rd TFW
Capt. Jon "JB" Kelk
Pennzoil 63

F-15C-40-MC 85-0125—aircraft destroyed: MiG-29; weapon: AIM-7M Sparrow; Tail Code: EG. The first MiG kill of the Gulf War was credited to Capt. Jon "JB" Kelk, flying number three position in Pennzoil flight. Pennzoil flight was part of an eight-ship MiG sweep in the western half of Iraq the first night of the war. Capt. Rick Tollini was Pennzoil lead, number two was Capt. Larry Pitts, number three was Capt. Jon Kelk, and number four was Capt. Steve Williams. An E-3 AWACS controller identified a flight of Iraqi fighters just north of Mudaysis closing fast on a flight of American F-15Es egressing from their targets. A second flight of MiGs popped up and was engaged by Pennzoil 63 (Kelk) and 64 (Williams). At first it was not clear to the F-15s if the second group of aircraft were MiGs or egressing American aircraft. The aircraft were quickly confirmed by an AWACS as hostile. "J.B." targeted one of the MiGs and launched an air-to-air missile. In the darkness he was not sure if the missile launched. The missile did in fact fire and was seen to hit and destroy a MiG-29 Fulcrum.

F-15C No. 85-0105, credited with two aerial victories on 17 January 1991, is seen postwar at Eglin AFB. During the mission of 17 January 1991, this F-15 was operating with the 58th Tactical Fighter Squadron (Gorillas). The 58th TFS was credited with the most aerial victories during the Gulf War. *P. Martian Collection*

7 January 1991
F-15C, No. 85-0105
58th TFS, 33rd TFW
Capt. Rob "Cheese" Graeter
Citgo 61

F-15C-39-MC 85-0105— aircraft destroyed: 2 Mirage F-1EQs; weapon: 2 AIM-7M Sparrows; Tail Code: EG. During the first mission of the Gulf War, Capt. Rob "Cheese" Greater was leading Citgo flight on a CAP. The captain was informed by an AWACS controller that Iraqi aircraft were being launched and was directed to intercept a flight of F-15Es that had just conducted an air strike against an Iraqi SCUD launching site. Capt. Greater and Citgo flight were positioned above the AWACS contacts when they identified them as enemy aircraft. The Iraqi aircraft were identified as Mirage F-1s and taken under attack by Citgo flight. During the intercept Capt. Greater engaged and destroyed two of the Iraqi Mirage F-1s.

17 January 1991
F-15C, 83-0017
71st TFS, 1st TFW
Capt. Steven "Tater" Tate
Quaker 11

F-15C-39-MC 83-0017—aircraft destroyed: Mirage F-1QE; weapon: 1 AIM-7M Sparrow; Tail Code: FF. During the first hours of the air strikes on Baghdad, for the most part the Iraqi Air Force attempted not to engage coalition CAP flights, but at least one Iraqi pilot decided to engage Capt. Steve "Tater" Tate of the 71st TFS, 1st TFW from Langley AFB, Virginia. Capt. Tate reported the Iraqi aircraft was closing on his F-15 when he "locked him in." Once he was positive it was hostile he fired a Sparrow missile that hit the approaching enemy Mirage. When last seen the Mirage "was a huge fireball."

1st TFW fighter 83-0017 in full afterburner takeoff on 19 March at Nellis AFB, Las Vegas, Nevada, and attached to the boom of a tanker during Red Flag Alaska. *B. Vissers & T. Miller Collections*

No. 85-0108 in a two-tone gray color scheme. The star and bars on the aircraft and the Tactical Air Command (TAC) emblem are depicted in color. During the Gulf War, all the markings on all USAF premier air superiority fighters were low visibility. *P. Martin Collection*

17 January 1991
F-15C, No. 85-0108
58th TFS, 33rd TFW
Capt. Rhory "Hoser"
**   Draeger**
Citgo 25

F-15C-40-MC 85-0108—aircraft destroyed: MiG-29; weapon: AIM-7M Sparrow; Tail Code: EG. On 17 January 1991, Capt. Rhory "Hoser" Draeger was flying F-15C No. 85-0108 when he claimed an aerial victory over an Iraqi MiG-29. During the MiG kill mission Capt. Draeger was flying CAP for a major air strike. The captain and his flight were sweeping out in front of a coalition strike package south of al-Taqaddum when they encountered heavy surface-to-air missile and anti-aircraft fire. While evading enemy air defenses Draeger acquired an enemy MiG-29, locked up the enemy aircraft, and selected an AIM-7M Sparrow that after launching tracked directly to the MiG and upon impact totally destroyed it. The strike package continued on to an airfield west of Baghdad. Tragically, Capt. Rhory "Hoser" Draeger of the 58th TFS, 33rd TFW was killed in March 1995 in a motor vehicle accident in Oregon.

On 17 January 1991, this MiG killer was flown by Capt. Charles Magill (USMC) when he destroyed an Iraqi MiG-29. Six years after the Gulf War, 85-0107 was still flying with the USAF. The tail code "EG" indicates the aircraft was assigned to Eglin AFB. While assigned to the 58th TFS this aircraft was involved in Northern Viking 97 air war exercises in Iceland. *P. Martin Collection*

17 January 1991
F-15C, No. 85-0107
58th TFS, 33rd TFW
Capt. Charles "Sly" Magill (USMC)
Zerex 71

F-15C-39-MC 85-0107—aircraft destroyed: MiG-29; weapon: AIM-7M Sparrow; Tail Code: EG. Capt. Charles "Sly" Magill was a Marine Corps pilot flying with the 58th TFS during the Gulf War. On 17 January 1991, he was leading a flight of eight F-15s on a MiG sweep. During the mission Zerex flight was informed by an E-3 AWACS that a pair of MiG-29s were south of al-Taqaddum airfield. Zerex 71 Capt. Magill maneuvered his flight toward the MiGs. The MiGs began a turn into the approaching Eagles, enabling Magill to lock up one of the MiGs; without hesitation he selected a Sparrow and pulled the trigger, launching the missile at the Iraqi MiG. "Scratch another MiG."

F-15C No. 85-0114 and three other F-15s from the 58th Fighter Squadron, Eglin AFB, Florida, were captured on 19 July 1995. The 58th FS jets were in Reykjavik, Iceland, to participate in Northern Viking air exercises. The first two aircraft in the line of four are 85-0114 and 85-0105, both double MiG killers from the Gulf War. If you look closely just below the forward part of the canopy on the fuselage you can see the two small green stars denoting the aerial victories. During the Gulf War, the Air Force did away with the old "Red Star" marking used during the Korean and Vietnam Wars to identify aircraft credited with an air-to-air combat victory. *J. Allen USAF Photograph*

The 20 mm cannon of 85-0114 is seen positioned in the ring wing root. This photograph was likely taken at her home base at Eglin. *P. Martin Collection*

19 January 1991
26 January 1991
F-15C, No. 85-0114
58th TFS, 33rd TFW
Capt. Cesar "Rico"
 Rodriguez Jr.
Chevron 25

F-15C-40-MC 85-0114—aircraft destroyed: 1 MiG-29; 1 MiG-23; weapon maneuvering; AIM-7M Sparrow; Tail Code: EG. On 19 January 1991, Capt. Cesar "Rico" Rodriguez was flying lead in Chevron flight when his wingman, Capt. Underhill, downed a MiG-29 with an AIM-7M. During the same air battle "Rico" engaged the wingman of the MiG-29 shot down by Underhill. In the ensuing high speed air battle Capt. Rodriguez maneuvered the Iraqi MiG into the desert floor. Capt. Underhill witnessed the crash and described it: "He impacts with his nose about ten degrees short of going vertical, so he was probably still pulling when he hit. There was a tremendous explosion and fireball….this guy must have rolled for a half mile across the desert floor."

During a CAP on 26 January 1991, Capt. Cesar "Rico" Rodriguez claimed his second MiG kill of the Gulf War. Flying as element lead in Citgo flight with Capt. Bruce Till on his wing, they were involved with the fireball that had already killed two MiG-29s. Capt. Tony Schiavi, who was a member of Citgo flight, described the Rodriguez kill: "Rodriguez and Till both have missiles in the air heading toward the third MiG. The MiG is making a hard right turn into us, to point at us. 'Rico's' missile wins the race and hits the MiG head on, and Till's missile flew through the fireball that resulted from the exploding MiG."

In a post-Gulf War photo at Luke AFB, Arizona, on 18 August 2006, 79-0021 wears the markings of the flagship of the 2nd Fighter Squadron. It proudly displays a green star on the fuselage below the canopy. The emblem of the Air Training Command is painted above the tail code on the tail of the aircraft. *P. Taris Collections*

19 January 1991
F-15C, No. 79-0021
32nd TFS, 32nd TFG
Lt. David G. "Abby"
   Sveden
Rambo 04

F-15C-24-MC 79-0021—aircraft destroyed: Mirage F-1EQ, weapon: AIM-7M Sparrow, Tail Code: CR. On a day (19 January 1991) that saw American F-15 Eagles down six Iraqi aircraft, Lt. Sveden was flying in the number four position in Rambo flight on the wing of Capt. David S. Prather. Rambo had launched from Incirlik Air Base, Turkey, as part of two F-15 four-ship flights on a sweep mission near Kirkuk Airfield, north of Baghdad. Rambo flight was vectored to intercept a flight of two Iraqi Mirage F-1s heading in their direction.

The enemy aircraft (call sign "Lion") was engaged at approximately seven to eight miles. Rambo 03 downed the lead Mirage with an AIM-7M. Lt. Sveden also used an AIM-7 to bag his Mirage. The missile was seen to impact and sever the tail section of the approaching bogie.

After a short visit to Jacksonville NAS Towers Field, Florida, on 31 October 2004, this MiG killer is departing and heading home. During the Gulf War, this historic F-15 was assigned to the 525th TFS / 36th TFW and on 19 January 1991, while part of Rambo flight, destroyed an F-1 Mirage with a single AIM-7M. Here 79-0069 is the new mount of the 33rd Tactical Fighter Wing commander. *A. Wright Collection*

19 January 1991
F-15C, No. 79-0069
525th TFS, 36th TFW
Capt. David S. "Spyro"
Prather
Rambo 03

F-15C-26-MC 79-0069—aircraft destroyed: Mirage F-1EQ; weapon: AIM-7M Sparrow, Tail Code: BT. During air operations on 19 January 1991, American intelligence intercepted radio traffic from a flight of Iraqi Mirage F-1s (call sign "Lion Flight"). The lead pilot was a major, while the wingman was a junior lieutenant. The two Iraqi pilots were apparently arguing whether or not to engage a flight of F-15s coming at them. The smarter of the two (major) wanted to make a run for it, but during their moment of indecision Rambo flight locked the pair of F-1s up. Capt. Prather, who was Rambo 03, launched his first missile that went "stupid," then followed up the first launch with a second at eight miles and a third Sparrow at seven miles. His second shot hit the lead Iraqi F-1, destroying the aircraft on impact. The second F-1 was downed by Capt. Sveden, whose missile cut the tail off the junior lieutenant's aircraft. Neither Iraqi pilot was seen to eject.

F-15C No. 85-0099, flown by Capt. Larry "Cheery" Pitts on 19 January 1991, is parked on the ramp with a number of other Eagles from the 58th TFS / 33rd TFW. The date and location are unknown, but it is suspected to be pre-Gulf War. This F-15 Eagle was lost on 10 June 1997 in an accident at Eglin AFB. *D. Brown Collection*

19 January 1991
F-15C, No. 85-0099
58th TFS, 33rd TFW
Capt. Larry "Cherry" Pitts
Citgo 22

F-15C-39-MC 85-0099—aircraft destroyed: MiG-25; weapon: AIM-7M Sparrow; Tail Code: EG. On 19 January 1991, Capt. Larry Pitts of the 58th TFS was part of a CAP supporting a SCUD hunting mission in the western part of Iraq. An AWACS aircrew operating in the area reported radar contact with a flight of MiGs attempting to intercept a large strike package heading for targets around Baghdad. Citgo flight leader Rick Tollini headed his flight toward the bandits. The enemy aircraft were well out of range and no intercept took place. Citgo flight was high when they detected a second fast moving flight of MiGs below them.

Flying in the number two position in Citgo flight, Capt. Larry Pitts engaged the MiGs. "The bandits were at 500 feet and doing 700 knots, five miles in front of me crossing left to right [west to east]." Pitts was able to position himself in the rear of the MiG identified as a Russian built MiG-25 Foxbat and launched four missiles at the maneuvering MiG. The missiles were launched in ripple order: AIM-9M, AIM-7M, AIM-9M, and AIM-7M. The last missile went right up the tailpipe of the MiG. The pilot was seen to eject.

F-15C No. 85-0101 parked on the ramp and buttoned up for the day in the two-tone gray, light gray / gloss bluish camouflage scheme. During August 1997, F-15s of the 58th Tactical Fighter Squadron (TFS) were involved in air Operation NORTHERN VIKING 97 in Keflavik, Iceland. *P. Martin Collection*

19 January 1991
F-15C, No. 85-0101
58th TFS, 33rd TFW
Capt. Richard "Kluso" Tollini

Citgo 21F-15C-39-MC 85-0101—aircraft destroyed: MiG-25; weapon: AIM-7M Sparrow; Tail Code: EG. During the first day of air operations Citgo flight engaged a flight of Iraqi MiG-25 Foxbats.

During the air battle Capt. Larry Pitts (Citgo 22) downed the first MiG-25 with an AIM-7. Meanwhile, Capt. Rick "Kluso" Tollini was heavily engaged with a second Foxbat.

Capt. Tollini described the shoot down in Lou Drendel's *And Kill MiGs* (Squadron / Signal Publication). "I could see two big afterburner plumes coming out the back of the thing, so I asked my flight: 'Hey is anybody in burner?' None of them were, and about that time, I noticed two pylons on each wing, so I knew it couldn't be an F-14 or F-15. I shot an AIM-9, which looked like it was going to miss, so I shot an AIM-7 which seemed to fly right up inside of him before detonating. There was just one huge fireball, and no pieces came out, so the airplane just disintegrated. I called: 'Splash,' and directed everybody out westbound!"

F-15C 85-0122, flown by Capt. Craig "Mole" Underhill during his MiG-29 kill of 19 January 1991, sits on the ramp at Eglin AAFB, Florida. *D. Brown Collection*

19 January 1991
F-15C, No. 85-0122
58th TFS, 33rd TFW
Capt. Craig "Mole"
**   Underhill**
Chevron 26

F-15C-40-MC 85-0122—aircraft destroyed: MiG-29; weapon: AIM-7M Sparrow; Tail Code: EG. Chevron flight was fragged to fly CAP to protect a High Value Airborne Assets flight. The flight lead was Capt. "Rico" Rodriguez, number two was Capt. Craig "Mole" Underhill, number three was Capt. Mike "Fish" Fisher, and the last member of the flight was Capt. Pat "Pat-O" Moylan.

During the CAP, Chevron flight intercepted radio traffic indicating Citgo flight—led by Capt. Rick Tollini—was engaging enemy aircraft attempting to attack a large flight of F-16s egressing the target area. In the meantime, an AWACS controller reported it had a radar contact for three groups of bandits attempting to intercept the egressing flight of F-16 Falcons.

"Rico" Rodriguez and "Mole" Underhill attempted to intercept the third flight, but broke off when the MiGs turned and ran for al Taqaddum. They no sooner broke off when they were informed two different MiGs were on their tail only thirteen miles away, heading directly for them at high speed. Chevron one and two punched off their wing tanks and turned into the MiGs. At approximately eight miles the bandits were declared hostile. Capt. Underhill immediately fired an AIM-7 at the approaching MiGs that impacted the lead MIG head-on. The MIG exploded into a huge fireball. The kill was called by Capt. Rodriguez "Splash one."

MiG killer 85-0104 at Shaw AFB on 6 February 1987. During 2009, F-15C No. 85-0104 participated in exercise Taliman Saber 2009. The tail code "ZZ" indicates the aircraft was no longer assigned to the 58th TFS, when it was credited with downing a MiG-23 Flogger with Capt. Tony Schiavi at the controls. In 2009, 85-0104 was transferred to the 18th Wing out of Kadena AFB, Okinawa, Japan. *M. Eadie Collection*

26 January 1991
F-15C, No. 85-0104
58th TFS, 33rd TFW
Capt. Anthony "Kimo" Schiavi
Citgo 26

F-15C-39-MC 85-0104—aircraft destroyed: MiG-23; weapon: AIM-7M Sparrow; Tail Code: EG. On 26 January 1991, Capt. Tony Schiavi was flying on the wing of Capt. Rhory Draeger in the number two position of a flight of four F-15Cs on a High Value Asset Combat Air Patrol (HVACAP). Citgo flight was tasked with protecting AWACS (call sign Cougar) western and (Buckeye) central, and tanker aircraft operating in support of air operations over Iraq.

Flying lead was Capt. Rhory Draeger, number three was Capt. Cesar Rodriguez, and number four was Capt. Bruce Till. Citgo flight was informed by AWACS operating in the area that a flight of four MiG-23 Floggers had just taken off from an Iraqi airfield. Citgo flight attempted to intercept the Floggers but was unable to intercept. A second flight of MiG-23s was picked up by radar from one of the AWACS air controllers departing H-2, the same Iraqi airfield from which the first flight launched.

While Citgo flight headed for the second flight of MiGs one of the enemy aircraft turned and headed back to H-2. At approximately thirty miles Citgo flight cleaned off their aircraft and prepared to engage the low flying MiG-23 Floggers. The MiGs were locked by the Eagle pilots at approximately twenty miles in the weapons engagement zone (WEZ). The first F-15 pilot to engage was flight leader Capt. Draeger. Capt. Schiavi (Citgo 26) engaged second, firing two AIM-7s at the number two MiG. The captain describes the kill: "My guy rolled out, headed right at me, when my first missile hit him head-on. The enemy airplane was literally vaporized, and my second missile flew right through the fireball." In just a matter of seconds all three Floggers were shot down, leaving the desert floor covered with MiG parts.

F-15C No. 85-0119 on the ramp at Elmendorf AFB, Anchorage, Alaska on 12 August 2006. By the tail markings, the MiG killer has been transferred from the 58th TFS to the 19th Fighter Squadron of Alaskan Air Command. Tucked under the wings are a pair of air-to-air missiles: one AIM-9 Sidewinder, and the second missile appears to be the newer AIM-120. This was the same aircraft flown by Capt. Draeger when he sent his MiG-29 plunging earthward after being struck by an AIM-7M. *C. Starnes Collection*

26 January 1991
F-15C, No. 85-0119
58th TFS, 33rd TFW
Capt. Rhory "Hoser"
  Draeger
Citgo 25

F-15C-40-MC 85-0119—aircraft destroyed: MiG-23; weapon: AIM-7M Sparrow; Tail Code: EG. Capt. Draeger was flight leader on 26 January 1991, when his flight was informed by an AWACS controller (call sign Cougar) that a flight of MiG-23s from airfield H-2 was approximately eighty miles away, heading northwest.

As the flight leader, Capt. Draeger set his flight up to intercept the approaching Floggers. The captain was the first member of Citgo flight to engage. He locked his first missile (AIM-7M) on the Iraqi aircraft, but the missile failed to fire. He immediately selected another Sparrow and fired. Capt. Schiavi, who was flying on the wing of Draeger, described what happened next: "Draeger's missile hit the first MiG and exploded. There was a fireball, and a lot of dust and dirt under the MiG. The MiG flew on for a short time before it exploded."

Capt. Powell's 84-0027 was reassigned to the 48th Fighter Wing, Royal Air Force Base Lakenheath, United Kingdom, after the war. While assigned to the 53rd TFS during the Gulf War, the Eagle was one of two 53rd TFS aircraft credited with two kills. Well after the war the jet was still marked with the two green kill stars. *G. Stedman Collection*

27 January 1991
F-15C, 84-0027
53rd TFS, 36th TFW
Capt. Benjamin "Coma"
  Powell
Opec 02

F-15C-38-MC 84-0027—aircraft destroyed: 2 Mirage F-1EQs; weapon: AIM-7M Sparrow; Tail Code: BT. The 53rd Tactical Fighter Squadron deployed to Al-Kjarj Air Base, Saudi Arabia, in January 1991. On 27 January 1991, Capt. Benjamin D. "Coma" Powell engaged two Iraqi Mirage F-1 delta winged fighters. Powell destroyed the enemy aircraft with AIM-7 Sparrows.

Capt. Denney's No. 84-0025 has been reassigned to the 1st Fighter Wing (FW), 71st Fighter Squadron (FS). After completing an air demonstration 21 May 2004 during the Andrews AFB open house the Eagle taxies past the show line. *G. Phelps Collection*

27 January 1991
F-15C, 84-0025
53rd TFS, 36th TFW
Capt. Jay "OP" Denney
Opec 01

F-15C-38-MC 84-0025—aircraft destroyed: 2 MiG-23s; weapon AIM-9 Sidewinder; Tail Code: BT. F-15C No. 84-0025 (like 85-0027) was deployed to Al-Kjarj Air Base, Saudi Arabia, in January 1991. On 27 January 1991, Capt. Jay "OP" Denney was Opec lead (in 85-0025) with Capt. Powell (in 84-0024) on his wing when they were vectored by an AWACS crew to intercept and engage four Iraqi aircraft. In a short dogfight both Eagles downed the four enemy aircraft. Capt. Denney was credited with two MiG-23 Floggers via AIM-9 Sidewinders.

No. 79-0022 at the yearly air show at Andrews AFB, assigned to the 1st Tactical Fighter Wing and part of the Air Force F-15 Demonstration Team. The camouflage scheme has been changed to a two tone light gray and light blue. Capt. "Muddy" Watrous flew this F-15 on 28 January 1991, when he was down to his last AIM-7. His fourth and last missile struck and destroyed an Iraqi MiG-23 Flogger. *G. Phelps Collection*

28 January 1991
F-15, No. 79-0022
525th TFS, 36th TFW
Capt. Donald S. "Muddy"
    Watrous
Bite 04

F-15C-24-MC 79-0022—aircraft destroyed: MiG-23; weapon: AIM-7M Sparrow, Tail Code: BT. Capt. Donald S. "Muddy" Watrous was flying a Barrier CAP mission in the skies over eastern Iraq. When informed by AWACS control that a pair of MiG-23s were making a run for the Iraq-Iran border, Capt. Watrous (call sign Bite 04) was flying on the wing of Capt. Gary Bauman when he engaged one of the MiGs. Capt. Watrous had to drop three of his AIM-7s when they malfunctioned. Unfortunately for the MIG the fourth Sparrow worked perfectly and tracked directly to the enemy aircraft. The MiG went down in a ball of flames.

Desert war veteran F-15C 85-0102 has been credited with three aerial victories during 1991; three green stars are clearly visible underneath the windscreen. On 29 April 2007 at Langley AFB, Virginia, the iconic jet joined the 1st Wing of the Air Combat Command demonstration team. *I. Lebowitz Collection*

29 January 1991
7 February 1991
F-15C, 85-0102
58th TFS, 36th TFW
Capt. David "Logger" Rose
Capt. Anthony Murphy
Chevron 17
Chevron 22

F-15C-39-MC 85-0102—aircraft destroyed: 1 MiG-23; 2 Su-20/22s; weapon: AIM-7M Sparrow; Tail Code: EG. During Operation DESERT STORM F-15C No. 85-0102 obtained three aerial victories. One of the kills was by Capt. David "Logger" Rose, downing a MiG-23 Flogger with one of his radar AIM-7 Sparrows. On 7 February 1991, Capt. Anthony Murphy would engage two Su-20/22 Fitters in the area of the Iraq/Iranian border. The Fitters were attempting to flee to Iran when Murphy gave chase and destroyed them with AIM-7s. Capt. Rick Persons also downed an Su-22 with an AIM-7 during the same encounter.

79-0078 against a bright blue sky, giving the impression of just hanging or floating in midair while returning from a Red Flag mission and turning on final for runway 3L. Taken post-Gulf War at Nellis AFB (24 October 2007), the jet still carries two green stars denoting Lt. Robert "Gigs" Hehemann's two kills on 6 February 1991. At the time of the Gulf War it flew with tail code BT of the 36th TFW. *P. Taris Collection*

6 February 1991
F-15C, No. 79-0078
53rd TFS, 36th TFW
Capt. Thomas "Vegas"
  Dietz
Zerex 71

F-15C-26-MC 79-0078—aircraft destroyed: 2 MiG-21s; weapons: 2 AIM-9M Sidewinders; Tail Code: BT. While Capt. Robert Hehemann was downing his two Su-25s fleeing Iraq, Capt. Tom "Vegas" Dietz was engaging two MiG-21s also attempting to make it to Iran. Capt. Dietz—flying from Al Kharid—engaged the MiGs near the border with Iran. He was able to maneuver his F-15 into an offensive positive advantage to engage the MiGs, and from approximately seven nautical miles launched his missiles. Both Sidewinders worked as advertised and homed on the MiGs, which exploded in flight. The two MiGs were observed to impact the ground. There were no chutes seen in any of the four kills. The only thing left was the smoldering wreckage of the MiGs on the desert floor.

F-15C No. 85-0124 in full afterburner during takeoff at Nellis AFB, Nevada, in November 1994. The aircraft was only marked with a single kill, adding to the question of whether Col. Parsons was credited with one or two kills. *B. Smith Collection*

6 February 1991
7 February 1991
F-15C, No. 85-0124
58th TFS, 33rd TFW
Col. Rick Parsons
Chevron 21

F-15C-40-MC 85-0124—aircraft destroyed: Su-20/22; weapon: AIM-7M Sparrow; Tail Code: EG. On 7 February 1991, Col. Rick Parsons was wing commander of the 33rd TFW. During a BARCAP (Barrier Combat Air Patrol; fighter cover between the strike force and any expected threat) he was credited with downing an Iraqi Su-20/22 Fitter. The Russian manufactured Fitter is capable of a maximum speed of 870 mph and is armed with two 30 mm Nudelman-Rikhter NR-30 cannon with 80 rounds per gun. The jet is also equipped with two under-wing launch rails for AA-8 Aphid air-to-air missiles.

The colonel was flying lead in Chevron flight with Capt. Anthony R. "ET" Murphy on his wing when they intercepted and downed Iraqi aircraft attempting to escape to Iran. The official record indicates Parsons and Murphy bagged three Su-22/20 Fitters with AIM-7M Sparrows, with a possible fourth also being downed. It is also unclear whether a MiG-23 Flogger was shot down during the engagement.

CENTCOM's award message originally referenced two kills each for Col. Parsons and Capt. Murphy.

On 29 September 2009, F-15C No. 80-0003 on approach to Kingsley Field, Portland, Oregon, home of the Redhawks. The single green star on the front fuselage signifies the aircraft's kill during DESERT STORM. *B. Shemley*

7 February 1991
F-15C, No. 83-0003
525th TFS, 36th TFW
Maj. Randy W. "Rotor"
  May
Killer 03

F-15C-27-MC 80-0003—aircraft destroyed: Mi-24; weapon: AIM-7M Sparrow; Tail Code: BT. Capt. Randy W. May of the 525th TFS / 36th TFW was flying as Killer 03 in Killer flight when he engaged an Iraqi Mi-24 attack helicopter. During the engagement Capt. May launched two AIM-7s outside ten nautical miles. The missiles hit and destroyed the Mi-24.

Desert war veteran F-15C 85-0102 has been credited with three aerial victories during 1991; three green stars are clearly visible underneath the windscreen. On 29 April 2007 at Langley AFB, Virginia, the iconic jet joined the 1st Wing of the Air Combat Command demonstration team. *I. Lebowitz Collection*

2 February 1991
F-15, No. 79-0074
4525th TFS, 36th TFW
Capt. Gregory P. "Dutch"
** Masters**
Rifle 01

F-15C-26-MC 79-0074—aircraft destroyed: IL-76; weapon: AIM-7M Sparrow; Gun (?); Tail Code: BT. The Russian Ilyushin IL-76 (NATO code name Candid) is a Soviet built and supplied large capacity transport aircraft. The IL-76 can obtain a maximum speed of 606 mph and can travel over 3,107 miles. The aircraft is armed with two 23 mm machine guns. On 2 February 1991, Capt. "Dutch" Masters (call sign Rifle 01) engaged an IL-76; downing of the enemy aircraft was confirmed by intelligence. There is some question as to how the Candid was shot down. A number of sources claim it was downed with an AIM-7M, while others claim it was the only gun kill for the F-15 during the war.

Gen. Horner, in the rules of engagement prior to air operation in DESERT STORM, insisted gun kills and strafing were to be avoided. Again, there are those that suspect Capt. Master may have been very leery to admit to the gun kill because of Air Force rules.

Double MiG killer 79-0074 climbs to the sky in full afterburner after takeoff. The light clouds and blue sky truly accent the beauty and power of the Eagle. *M. Durning Collection*

6 February 1991
F-15C, No. 84-0019
53rd TFS, 36th TFW
Lt. Robert "Gigs"
   Hehemann
Zerex 54

F-15C-38-MC 84-0019—aircraft destroyed: 2 Su-25s; weapon: 2 AIM-9M Sidewinders; Tail Code: BT. On 6 February 1991, F-15s of the 53rd TFS, 36th TFW were fragged to fly CAP, attempting to locate and intercept Iraqi aircraft bugging out to Iran. Lt. Robert Hehemann (Zerex 54) and Capt. Dietz made contact with four bandits approximately sixty nautical miles northwest of their position. The bandits were fast movers, down low and heading for the border. "Gigs" Hehemann engaged two Iraqi Air Force Su-25 Frogfoot attack aircraft at approximately eight to nine nautical miles. Selected AIM-9M Sidewinders obtained a good tone, indicating the heat seekers in the noses of the missiles had locked on to the target. Both of the Sidewinders tracked directly to the fleeing enemy aircraft. The impact of the missiles caused the total destruction of the enemy Su-25.

Here 79-0048 is equipped with wing and centerline fuel tanks, a sure indication the aircraft is going on a long flight. With canopy open and crew ladder and crew chief in place, the only thing missing is the pilot. On 11 February 1991, Capt. Steve B. Dingee downed an Mi-8 during an air encounter, noted on the fuselage below the cockpit by an Iraqi national flag. *P. Martin Collection*

No. 79-0048 climbs into a blue sky on 22 April 2006 over the Florida panhandle while deployed with the 1st Fighter Wing "Fightin Furies" at Tyndall AFB, Florida. *J. Derden – Jetwash Collection*

11 February 1991
F-15C / No. 79-0048
525th TFS / 36th TFW
Capt. Steve B. "Gunga" Dingee
Pistol 01

F-15C-25-MC 79-0048—aircraft destroyed: Mi-8; weapon: AIM-7M Sparrow; Tail Code: BT. On day twenty-six of the war two F-15Cs from the 525th TFS joined forces to down an Iraqi attack helicopter in an area west of Mosul. Capt. Steve Dingee (call sign Pistol 01) and Capt. Mark McKenzie (call sign Pistol 02) each fired an AIM-7M at the same attack helicopter, which exploded in midair. Both Dingee and McKenzie were awarded half a kill for downing the Iraqi attack helicopter.

On 11 February 1991, F-15C No. 80-0012's call sign was Pistol 02 in Pistol flight when Capt. Mark McKenzie used an AIM-7M to help destroy an enemy attack helicopter in midair. On this overcast day 85-0012 is seen taxiing in preparation for takeoff. *P. Martin Collection*

11 February 1991
F-15C, No. 80-0012
525th TFS, 36th TFW
Capt. Mark McKenzie
Pistol 02

F-15C-27-MC 80-0012—aircraft destroyed: Mi-8; weapon: AIM-7M Sparrow; Tail Code: BT. See Narrative 11 February 1991, No. 79-0048.

F-15E No. 89-0487 at Bagrahm Air Field in Afghanistan, armed for a close air support mission. If one looks closely on the right side of the aircraft you can see the green star painted on the fuselage in recantation of the Bennett / Bakke kill of 14 February 1991. *USAF photograph by J. D'Angina*

14 February 1991
F-15E, No. 89-0487
335th TFS, 4th TFW
Capt. Richard T. Bennett
Capt. Dan B. Bakke
Packard 41

F-15E-47-MC 89-0487—aircraft destroyed: Mi-24; weapon: GBU-10; Tail Code: SJ. One of the most unusual aerial victories of the Gulf War occurred when an American F-15E Strike Eagle downed an Iraqi helicopter with one of its GBU-10s (2,000 lb. LGBs). Capt. Richard T. Bennett and his WSO, Capt. Daniel B. Bakke, were operating in northwestern Iraq on a SCUD killing mission in the area of airfield H-2. Their flight was alerted by an AWACS to the presence of Iraqi helicopters operating in the vicinity of American troops on the ground. The AWACS confirmed no friendly aircraft operating in the area and cleared Packard flight to engage and fire on the enemy aircraft.

Bennett and Bakke's F-15E Strike Eagle was armed with four GBU-10s and four AIM-9 Sidewinders when they located and identified the helicopters as Russian Mi-24 Hinds. The enemy helos were on the ground, in the process of dropping off Iraqi troops, when Bennett and Bakke targeted one of the enemy aircraft with a GBU-10 LGB. While lasing the target the Hind started to take off. Bennett and Bakke kept lasing the target while it hovered in the area. The 2,000 pound bomb was released and impacted, and the detonation destroyed the helicopter.

In a postwar interview, Capt. Bennett described the results of the attack: "There was a big flash, and I could see pieces flying in different directions. It blew the helicopter to hell, damn near vaporized it."

F-15C No. 84-0014 in full afterburner taking off from RAF Lakenheath, England, on 19 August 2005. In the thirty-eight-day air campaign one hundred and twenty F-15s deployed flew over 5,900 sorties. *R. Powney Collection*

20 March 1991
F-15C, No. 84-0014
53rd TFS, 36th TFW
Capt. John T. Doneski
Amoco 34

F-15C-37-MC 84-0014—aircraft destroyed: Su-22M; weapon: AIM-9M Sidewinder; Tail Code: BT. The shooting war in Iraq was officially ended on 28 February 1991, but the Iraqi military was intent on carrying out air and ground operations against anyone opposing the government. On 20 March 1991, Capt. John T. Doneski of the 53rd TFS / 36th TFW was on CAP with a second F-15 Eagle north of Baghdad enforcing the no fly zone. The pair of F-15s from Amoco flight was alerted to the presence of Iraqi Su-22s operating in violation of the no fly zone. The two aircraft were intercepted over Tikrit by F-15s of the 53rd TFS. Capt. Doneski positively identified the two aircraft, then engaged the trailing Fitter, armed an AIM-9 Sidewinder, and after obtaining a strong tone launched the missile. The Sidewinder tracked directly to the enemy aircraft, destroying it in flight.

Operation SOUTHERN WATCH

Shortly after expelling (28 February 1991) Iraqi military forces from Kuwait, Joint Task Force Southeast Asia (JTF-SWA) imposed Operation SOUTHERN WATCH, consisting of armed fighter sweeps established to monitor and control the airspace over southern Iraq following the Gulf War. Two days after Christmas 1992, Iraqi aircraft challenged coalition aircraft enforcing the no fly zone when they sent two MiG-25 Foxbats below the 32nd parallel, threatening USAF aircraft. One of the threatening Foxbats was quickly engaged by an F-16 Falcon piloted by Lt. Col. Gary L. North, who dispatched the Foxbat with a single AIM-120 (AMRAMM).

On 20 and 22 March 1991, American F-15s shot down three additional Iraqi aircraft that ventured into the no fly zone. Two single seat, ground attack Su-22 Fitters and one Pilatus PC-9 were credited to the 53rd Tactical Fighter Squadron (TFS).

24 March 1999
F-15C, No. 84-0014
493rd FS, 48th FW
Capt. Cesar "Rico"
Rodriguez Jr.

F-15C-37-MC 84-0014—aircraft destroyed: MiG-29; weapon: AIM-120C; Tail Code LN. The first night of Operation ALLIED FORCE in the Balkans, Capt. Rodriguez was flying in a MiGCAP flight when a number of MiG-29s rose to counter the initial NATO air strikes. Two of the Floggers came from Nis Air Force Base. The first of two MiGs was engaged by a Dutch F-16 Falcon that damaged the MiG with an AIM-120. The second MiG-29, flown by Maj. Lijo Arizanov, was engaged by Capt. Rodriguez. During the engagement Maj. Arizanov was struggling to engage his radar when a missile fired by Rodriquez struck and destroyed his Flogger.

This was Capt. Cesar Rodriguez' third and final kill of his career. The captain shot down two MiGs during the Gulf War, making him one of the leading MiG killers since the Vietnam War. The F-15 flown by Rodriguez during 24 March 1999 (F-15C Tail Number 84-0014) is the only F-15 credited with an aerial victory during Operations DESERT STORM and ALLIED FORCE.

48th Fighter Wing / 493rd Tactical Fighter Squadron F-15C No. 84-0014 was credited with downing a Serbian MiG-29 on 3 March 1999. To date No. 84-0014 is the only USAF F-15C credited with kills in two different conflicts. *G. Stedman Collection*

No. 84-0010 on final approach to RAF Lakenheath, England. On 24 October 2013, the Eagle was assigned to the 36th TFW when flown by Capt. Thomas "Vegas" Dietz during his aerial victory over an Iraqi Su-22 Fitter. It was 84-0010's first kill and the third for Dietz. *G. Stedman Collection*

22 March 1991
F-15C, No. 84-0010
53rd TFS, 36th TFW
Capt. Thomas "Vegas"
** Dietz**
Zerex 21

F-15C-37-MC 84-0010—aircraft destroyed: Su-22M; weapon: AIM-9M Sidewinder; Tail Code: BT. The Gulf War officially ended on 28 February 1991, but United States and coalition air forces maintained a no fly zone in parts of northern and southern Iraq. On 20 March 1991, American F-15s tasked with enforcing the no fly zone made radar contact with two Iraqi aircraft operating in violation of the zone. First contact was made by radar, placing the targets thirty some miles away from Zerex flight. Zerex lead Capt. Thomas "Vegas" Dietz and his wingman, Lt. "Digs" Hehemann, were cleared to engage the bandits after it was established the two aircraft were operating in the no fly zone in violation of the rules of engagement (ROE). It was further established that the Iraqi aircraft had no business being in the area when they were detected. The two enemy aircraft were heading west at approximately fifteen nautical miles when Capt. Dietz identified one of the aircraft as an Iraqi Su-22 Fitter. He selected and armed one of his AIM-9s; once the missile locked on the target he launched the missile. Capt. Dietz stated after the mission: "The missile came off the rail and flew right up the tailpipe of the Fitter. It blew up just like you see in the movies. I had to maneuver to avoid the fireball."

22 March 1991
F-15C, No. 84-0015
53rd TFS, 36th TFW
Lt. Robert "Gigs" Hehemann
Zerex 22

F-15C-37-MC 84-0015—aircraft destroyed: PC-9; weapon: Maneuvering; Tail Code: BT. Intelligence indicated the two aircraft intercepted by Zerex flight on 22 March 1991 were on their way home from a bombing mission against the Kurds in northern Iraq. The Su-22 Fitter was taken out by an AIM-9M Sidewinder fired by Capt. Thomas Dietz. The second aircraft in the enemy flight was a turboprop Pilatus PC-9 acting as a forward air controller (FAC), picking out Kurdish targets for the Fitter.

Capt. Robert Hehemann approached the PC-9 in an attempt to intimidate the pilot. Without Hehemann firing a shot at the enemy aircraft, the Iraqi pilot ejected from the aircraft and was seen in his chute on the way down.

F-15C No. 84-0015 well after the Gulf War and clearly depicting the brute power and graceful lines of the Eagle. It was taken on 25 October 2005 while the Eagle was being repaired at RAF Lakenheath. The air brake has been deployed as it approaches runway 24. The second photograph was taken with a 50 mm lens just as the Eagle passed overhead, ready to touch down. *K. Drage / W. Houquet Collections*

Operation ALLIED FORCE

On 24 March 1999, the North Atlantic Treaty Organization (NATO), operating under its own flag, began military operations against the Federal Republic of Yugoslavia. The mission—code-named Operation ALLIED FORCE by NATO and Operation NOBLE ANGLE by the United States—was the first time NATO used military force without the approval of the United Nations Security Council.

The bombing campaign conducted during Operation ALLIED FORCE sought to stop human rights abuse in Kosovo. A very important part of the campaign involved air combat between F-15s and F-16s of NATO and the Yugoslavian Air Force. The overwhelming advantage in the air campaign was quickly established by NATO with the deployment of over 1,031 combat aircraft. NATO aircraft were deploying mostly from air bases in Italy or aircraft carriers stationed in the Adriatic.

During Operation ALLIED FORCE, the Yugoslavian Air Force was ill equipped to meet the challenge presented by NATO; at the time Yugoslavia only had 46 combat capable MiG-21s augmented with 16 MiG-29s.

When NATO launched the air campaign element of Operation ALLIED FORCE on 24/25 March 1999, the Yugoslavian Air Force scrambled 5 MiG-29 Floggers that were vectored to intercept NATO aircraft over southern Serbia and Kosovo. The Floggers were quickly dealt with by F-15s from the 493rd Fighter Squadron. One of the MiGs was damaged by an AIM-120, while a second was shot down by Capt. Cesar "Rico" Rodriguez Jr. As the air campaign evolved, six of Yugoslavia's 16 MiG-29s were shot down or crashed, while another four were destroyed on the ground. F-15s claimed an additional 3 MiG-29s in air combat: a second on 24 March credited to Capt. Michael "Dozer" Shower and a double MiG-29 kill on 26 March by Capt. Jeffery C. J. Hwang.

24 March 1999–10 June 1999

24 March 1999
F-15C, No. 86-0159
493rd FS, 48th FW
Capt. Michael "Dozer"
   Shower
Unknown

F-15C-41-MC 86-0159—aircraft destroyed: MiG-29; weapon: AIM-120C Slammer; Tail Code: LN. Batajnica airfield is north of Belgrade and has been used for years as a MiG fighter base. On 24 March 1999, Capt. Michael Shower of the 493rd Expeditionary Fighter Squadron was on patrol in the area of Batajnica, tasked with protecting a strike force. The captain had been briefed prior to launch that there would be F-117 Nighthawks operating in the area. Shortly after Lt. Col. Rodriguez engaged and downed an enemy MiG, Capt. Shower locked on to an unidentified aircraft on its way out of Batajnica airfield. The MiG was detected closing on Shower when he was cleared to fire. He launched two AIM-120s, both of which failed to hit the target. Unbeknownst to the captain, one of four friendly F-117s was positioned between him and the MiG.

The F-117 pilot was at only 2,000 feet and just below Shower when he fired his two missiles. The Stealth pilot thought he was being fired on when he first saw the two missiles.

After reacquiring the MiG, Capt. Shower again locked on with another air-to-air missile and fired. The third missile tracked directly to the enemy aircraft and impacted with a violent explosion. The MiG-29s engaged by Capt. Shower were operating from Batajnica Air Base. Showers' AIM-120 missile destroyed the Flogger being flown by Maj. Nebojsa Nikolic. The major was able to eject from his stricken aircraft and survived the engagement.

On 24 March 1999, Capt. Michael Shower was flying 86-0159 when he engaged and destroyed a MiG-29 flown by Maj. Nebojsa Nikolic from the 127th Lovacka Avijacijska Eskadrila (fighter squadron), known as *Vitezovi* (Knights). The aircraft is taxiing after a training sortie in the United Kingdom. Note the nose MiG kill marking for its MiG-29 kill during Operation ALLIED FORCE. *C. Lofting / G. Stedman Collections*

F-15C No. 86-0169 was lost when it crashed on 26 March 2001 near the summit of Ben Macdui, in the Cairngorm Mountains, Scotland. Also lost in the same accident was F-15C No. 86-0180. Pilots Lt. Col. Kenneth John Hyvonen and Capt. Kirk Jones were killed. *P. Martin Collection*

24 March 1999
F-15C, No. 86-0169
493rd EFS, 48th FW
Capt. Cesar "Rico"
** Rodriguez**
Knife 13

F-15C-41-MC 86-0169—aircraft destroyed: 1 MiG-29; weapon: AIM-120A Slammer; Tail Code: LN. On 24 March 1999, Capt. Cesar "Rico" Rodriguez would claim his third MiG (in 86-0169), making him the highest scoring American pilot since the Vietnam War.

During Operation ALLIED FORCE the captain shot down a Serbian MiG-29 flown by Maj. Llijo Arizanon with an AIM-120A advanced medium range air-to-air missile (AMRAM). The AIM-120A is a beyond visual range air-to-air (BVRAAM) missile.

F-15C No. 85-0156 breaks right on approach to RAF Coringsby, United Kingdom. The 439rd Fighter Squadron (FS) was participating in a joint exercise (YANKEE IMPORT) with 11 Squadron of the RAF. *G. Stedman Collection*

26 March 1999
F-15C, No. 86-0156
493rd FS, 48th FW
Capt. Jeffrey C. J. Hwang
Dirk 01

F-15C-41-MC 86-0156—aircraft destroyed: 2 MiG-29s; weapon: 2 AIM-120A Slammers; Tail Code: LN. Capt. Jeffrey C. J. Hwang and Capt. J. "Boomer" McMurray deployed with the 48th Fighter Wing from Lakenheath AFB, England, in support of Operation ALLIED FORCE. During a MiGCAP mission on 26 March 1999, Capt. Hwang was flying lead in Dirk flight with "Boomer" McMurray on his wing. Dirk flight was alerted to two hostile aircraft operating in their patrol area in clear disregard of NATO directives.

Hwang and the E-3 Sentry AWACS controller (call sign Magic 77) both established radar contact with the bandits, which were identified as Serbian MiG-29s.

The two MiG-29 Fulcrums were being piloted by Lt. Col. Slobodan Peric and Capt. 1st Class Zoran Radosavljevic when they were engaged by Hwang and McMurray. In the heat of combat things have a tendency to get confused and it is not quite clear who engaged the MiGs first, as both crews launched air-to-air missiles at the approaching MiGs. Official Air Force records indicate two AIM-120s fired by Capt. Hwang took out the two Fulcrums.

Rounding out the Final Gulf War Score

There is no doubt coalition F-15s ended the Gulf War as the premier dogfighters of the air campaign, but they were not the only coalition aircraft credited with aerial combat victories. The history of the air campaign also identifies six additional kills that contributed significantly to the air war and in fact made aviation history. Credited to the United States Navy were F/A-18s (2 kills) and an F-14 Tomcat (1 kill), while the USAF an EF-111 (1 kill) and an A-10A (2 kills).

17 January 1991
F/A-18C, BuNo 163508
USS Saratoga (CV-60),
VFA-81 Sunliners
Lt. Cmdr. Mark I. "MRT"
Fox
Quicksand 64

F/A-18C-25-MC 163508—aircraft destroyed: F-7A MiG-21 Fishbed; weapon: AIM-9 Sidewinder AAM. On 17 January 1991, Lt. Mark I. Fox and his wingman, Lt. Commander Nick Mongillo, launched from the USS *Saratoga* on a bombing mission to an Iraqi airfield in southwest Iraq. Both F/A-18 Hornets were armed with four 2,000 lb. bombs. While en route they were contacted by a Navy E2C that stated two MiGs were approaching at a fast rate of speed. Quicksand flight (Fox and Mongillo) located the enemy MiGs and were able to engage, fire on, and destroy them without ejecting their bombs. The flight then continued to attack the Iraqi airfield. Lt. Cmdr. Fox would claim the first aerial victory for the F/A-18 Hornet.

After landing at Coringsby, the F-15 Eagle flown by Capt. Jeffrey C. J. "Claw" Hwang during his double MiG kill mission is seen taxiing during Exercise YANKEE IMPORT. *G. Stedman Collection*

Lt. Commander Mark I. Fox, while flying F/A-18 Hornet BuNo 163508 from the USS *Saratoga* (CV-60), made aviation history when he shot down an Iraqi F-7A (MiG-21 Fishbed). The kill was the first in history for the Hornet. *R.B. Greby via D. F. Brown*

17 January 1991
F/A-18C, BuNo 163502
USS Saratoga (CV-60),
    VFA-81 Sunliners
Lt. Cmdr. Nick "Mongo"
    Mongillo
Quicksand 62

F/A-18C-25-MC 163502—aircraft destroyed: F-7A MiG-21 Fishbed; weapon: AIM-7 Sparrow AAM. See Narrative F/A-18 BuNo 163508.

This F/A-18C Hornet was credited with the second F/A-18 MiG kill during Operation DESERT STORM, when Lt. Commander Nick Mongillo shot down an Iraqi F-7A. Here it is at Naval Air Station Cecil Field, Florida, in May 1991. *D. F. Brown Collection*

Another American aircraft that made aviation history during the war was EF-111 Raven tail number 66-0016, when the aircrew—Capt. James Denton and his WSO, Capt. Brent Brandon—were attacked by an Iraqi Mirage F-1. Turning the tables on the Mirage, the Raven aircrew outmaneuvered the enemy aircraft, forcing it to crash. In September 1983, the historic EF-111 was at Mountain Home AFB, Idaho. Today the Raven (also nicknamed Spark Vark) sits on display outside the main gate at Cannon AFB, Clovis, New Mexico. *G. Helmer Collection*

17 January 1991
EF-111A, No. 66-0016
390th ECS, 366th TFW
Capt. James Denton
Capt. Brent "Brandini"
**   Brandon**

General Dynamics EF-111 (Raven) 66-0016—aircraft destroyed; Mirage F-1; weapon: maneuver. During the early morning hours of 17 January 1991, the coalition launched Operation DESERT STORM against Saddam Hussein and the Iraqi military. Approximately 22 F-15E Strike Eagles led by EF-111 electronic warfare aircraft were approaching Iraqi airfields H-3 and H-4 when Iraqi Mirage F-1s attempted to intercept the bomb laden Strike Eagles. Capts. James Denton and Brent "Brandin" Brandon (in EF-111 66-0016) were engaged by one of the Iraqi Mirage fighters. During the high speed aggressive, low level engagement Denton and Brandon were able to outmaneuver the Iraqi jet, forcing it to impact with the ground.

Not known for its dogfighting capabilities, this Warthog (tail no. 77-0205) had the distinction of being the first A-10A credited with an aerial victory. Here it is armed with AIM-9 Sidewinders, but the kill credited to this A-10 was accomplished with the 30 mm cannon. *Sgt. K. Foy via D. F. Brown*

6 February 1991
A-10A, No. 77-0205
706th TFS, 926th TFG
Capt. Robert "Swaino"
** Swan**
Savage 01

Fairchild Republic A-10A (Thunderbolt) 77-0205—aircraft destroyed: BO-105; weapon: GAU-8 Gatling gun. Capt. Robert "Swaino" Swan of the 706th TFW had just attacked two Iraqi tanks with Maverick missiles in central Kuwait when he observed strange movement some distance from his position. Swan said: "They weren't putting up any dust and were moving fast over the desert." One of the coalition forward air control aircraft (FAC) confirmed the fast moving object was in fact an Iraqi helicopter. Capt. Swan attempted to engage the aircraft with an AIM-9 Sidewinder, but the missile would not lock on the target. Switching to the Warthog's 30 mm, seven barrel cannon, he attacked the helicopter. During the first pass he fired approximately 30 rounds; during a second pass he unloaded approximately 300 rounds, at which time the aircraft just fell apart. "It looked like it was hit with a bomb."

Close-up of the nose of A-10A 77-0205 *Chopper Popper*, proclaiming the A-10A's combat history while deployed for DESERT STORM. *Sgt. K. Foy via D. F. Brown*

F-14A Tomcat BuNo 162603 (in June 1991) was the only Tomcat credited with an aerial victory (Mi-8 Hip) during DESERT STORM. *J. Puzzullo via D. F. Brown*

6 February 1991
F-14A, BuNo 162603
USS Range r (CV-61),
 VFA-1 Wolfpack
Lt. Stuart "Meat" Broce
Commander Ron "Bongo"
 McElraft
Wichita 103

Grumman F-14-135-GR 162603—aircraft destroyed: Mi-8 Hip; weapon: AIM-9S Sidewinder AAM. During the Gulf War, United States Navy F-14 Tomcats were tasked mainly to defensive CAPs for the fleet, but on occasion the Tomcat would venture into enemy territory when escorting strike aircraft. On 6 February 1991, Lt. Stuart Broce and Cmdr. Ron McElraft (flying from the USS *Ranger* [CV-61] in F-14A BuNo 162603) engaged, fired on, and destroyed an Iraqi Hi-8 Hip helicopter with a single AIM-9S air-to-air missile.

A-10A tail number 81-0964 was the second Thunderbolt credited with an aerial victory. Capt. "Shanghai" Sheehy destroyed an Iraqi Mi-8 Hip helicopter with the aircraft's 30mm cannon. Prior to DESERT STORM, the A-10 was a much maligned beast, but the Warthog would emerge from its first combat as one of the most feared weapons of the war. *Sgt. K. Foy via D.F. Brown*

15 February 1991
A-10A, No. 81-0964
511th TFS, 10th TFW
Capt. Todd "Shanghai"
Sheehy

Fairchild Republic A-10A (Thunderbolt) 81-0964—aircraft destroyed: Mi-8; weapon: GAU-8 Gatling gun. While on his twenty-seventh combat sortie Capt. "Shanghai" Sheehy from the 511th TFS, King Fahd Airport, Kifa, Saudi Arabia, identified an Iraqi Mi-8 Hip helicopter in his area of operation. The captain reacted quickly and engaged the Iraqi aircraft with his A-10A 30 mm cannon. The Mi-8 was totally destroyed in the encounter. This would be the second aerial combat victory for the A-10A Thunderbolt.

CHAPTER 9

GENERAL DYNAMICS (NOW LOCKHEED MARTIN) F-16 "NETZ," "BARAK"

The "First Jet" Squadron—Knights of the North

F-16A/B Netz (Sparrowhawk)

The F-16/A/B models entered service with the IASF "First Jet" Squadron approximately four years after F-15s entered service with Double Tail Squadron. Known as the F-16 Falcon or Viper in the United States and NATO Air Forces, the F-16 would become known in the IASF as the Netz (Sparrowhawk).

Originally designed as a lightweight fighter, in service with the IASF the F-16A/B Netz quickly evolved into a true multi-role aircraft, equally capable of air-to-air or air-to-ground missions.

The first 75 F-16 Netz appeared in the IASF in July 1980, joining the "First Jet" Squadron. The second squadron, Knights of the North, arrived in September 1980. Both of these squadrons operate out of Ramat David Air Base near the Syria and Lebanon borders.

Two signature events defined the F-16 Netz as a true multi-role fighter, and one was the most publicized combat mission of the F-16: on 7 June 1981, an air strike took out the "jewel in the crown" of President Saddam Hussein's nuclear program. Eight F-16 Netz from the "First Jet" Squadron and the Knights of the North successfully flew from Etzion Air Base to the nuclear reactor at Al Tuwaitha Nuclear Center near Baghdad, delivering their ordnance on target, destroying the nuclear reactor, and returning safely home. The second is their performance in the Lebanon War in 1982, when F-16s and F-4Es were tasked with the destruction of the entire Soviet designed Syrian air defense system. Within a matter of hours the IASF, led by the F-16s of the IASF, totally devastated the surface-to-air missile systems without a single aircraft loss. Seventeen of nineteen surface-to-air batteries were destroyed the first day. The IASF Sparrowhawk also demonstrated its air-to-air capabilities, destroying approximately twenty-nine SyAAF MiG-21s and -23s during the first days of air combat over the Beqaa Valley.

The F-16 Netz, like the F-15 Baz, claimed its first aerial combat victory while engaged in the skies of the Middle East. The first kill was achieved by Rafi Raz on 28 April 1981, when he downed a SyAAF Mi-8 helicopter with the internal 20 mm cannon of his F-16. On 14 July 1981, Amir Nahumi downed the first fixed wing aircraft when he engaged, fired on, and destroyed a SyAAF MiG-21. The Sparrowhawk of the IASF would not claim another aerial combat victory until 1 April 1982, when Ze'ev Raz destroyed a MiG-23 Flogger of the SyAAF.

F-16 Netz over Lebanon

The IASF F-16A/B Netz has proven itself a most capable air-to-ground and air-to-air weapon system in the hands of Israeli pilots. The Netz has been deployed by the IASF in air-to-ground missions against surface-to-air missile sites, radar sites, troop concentrations, airfields, armored vehicles, command and control centers, communication centers, etc., while amassing quite an impressive air-to-air combat record. In the skies over Lebanon during 1981–1982, F-16s of the IASF claimed over forty aerial victories over Syrian Arab Air Force fighters. The F-16 Barak and F-16I Sufa (2006–2013) have also been credited with the destruction of at least four Iranian manufactured UAVs (Unmanned Aerial Vehicles) launched by Hezbollah.

Aerial Combat Victories
F-16 Netz, Barak
28 April 1981
F-16A, No. 126
"First Jet" Squadron, IASF
Dubi Yoffe

F-16A-Block 5 78-0321 No. 126—aircraft destroyed: 1 Mi-8; weapon AIM-9L Sidewinder. The "First Jet" Squadron's F-16A Netz No. 126 was flown by Dubi Yoffe on 28 April 1981 when he claimed the second Mi-8 kill in the area of Jebel Snin.

F-16A Netz No. 126 in full afterburner takeoff into a clear blue Middle Eastern sky. Netz 126 tail markings show it is now assigned to Flying Wing Squadron of the IASF, but on 28 April 1981, this aircraft was deployed with the "First Jet" Squadron when it was credited with downing a Syrian Mi-8 helicopter with a single AIM-9L Sidewinder. *O. Zidon Collection*

With aerial kill markings painted on its nose, No. 112 is in full afterburner takeoff from Ovda Air Base. Ovda Air Base is said to be in a great location for an active military training base. The aircraft appears with the new Flying Wing Squadron emblem painted on the tail. *O. Zidon Collection*

28 April 1981
Ra'am, Thunder
F-16A, No.112
"First Jet" Squadron, IASF
Maj. Rafi Berkovich
Itzhak Gat

F-16A-Block 5 78-0314 No. 112—aircraft destroyed: 1 Mi-8; 1 DR-3 Drone; weapon: M-61 Vulcan 20 mm cannon; AIM-9 Sidewinder air-to-air missile. "We suddenly heard an earsplitting siren wail. We ran like madmen to our planes, revved them up, and took off."

The flight of F-16s had been scrambled to investigate Syrian helicopters operating in the area of Jebel Snin. Approximately ten miles from Riak airfield, shortly after take-off Maj. Berkovich established radar contact with an unidentified aircraft. The rules of engagement required the target be positively identified before permission would be granted to engage. While waiting for permission to launch Maj. Berkovich lost his radar lock on the unidentified aircraft.

A short time passed before Rafi Berkovich reacquired the target on radar and he was now authorized to engage. At minimum range, Berkovich launched an air-to-air missile at the target.

"The missile left the plane with a whoosh, and I followed it with my glance. It veered downward, hit the ground and entered a small shack, and sent it up in the air. Later that day, the announcer on the news said 'our forces had fired rockets in the area.'" Well, those so-called rockets were my misguided missile and nothing else.

Rafi Berkovich switched to cannon sights and went after the helicopter in a diving attack. Pulling in on the six o'clock position of the target, he fired. The helicopter was seen trailing heavy black smoke before crashing. (IASF official website)

Netz 219 (here perhaps at Nevatim) was flown by the Knights of the North on 14 July 1981, when Amir Nahumi downed a SyAAF MiG-21. Nestled in the wing root where the wing and fuselage merge is the internal 20 mm M61 Vulcan cannon. Here Netz 219 has been reassigned to Golden Eagle Squadron, the first IASF squadron to introduce the new tail art that now appears on many IASF jets. *A. Dor Collection*

14 July 1981
F-16A, No. 219
Knights of the North Squadron, IASF
Amir Nahumi

F-16A-Block 10 78-0326 No. 219—aircraft destroyed: 1 MiG-21; weapon: AIM-9L Sidewinder. The summer of 1981 was a time of heightened tensions between Israel and Syria. The Syrians had been detected moving troops into the Jebel Snin area. On 14 July 1981, Amir Nahumi of the Knights of the North claimed the first fixed wing aerial victory for the F-16 when he engaged, fired on, and destroyed a SyAAF MiG-21. Now a retired brigadier general, Amir Nahumi amassed quite a combat record during his service with the IASF. The general downed four Syrian MiG-17s on his very first combat mission while an F-4E Phantom II pilot. He would go on to claim four additional MiGs in the Phantom II. In 1982, he would claim five more kills in the F-16, making him the first F-16 Netz ace in history.

No. 219 stands ready to respond to any enemy intruder that may enter Israeli airspace. The aircraft is configured with four Sidewinders. Golden Eagle Squadron, like many other squadrons, maintains aircraft in hardened shelters all over Israel. *O. Zidon Collection*

Prior to Hagai Katz' MiG kill of 21 April 1982, he was already an accomplished fighter pilot, having participated in the historic 7 June 1981 air strike against the Iraqi nuclear reactor during Operation OPERA. During OPERA Katz flew in Eshkol flight as Eshkol 04. Here No. 284 is being prepared for a night launch. *O. Zidon Collection*

21 April 1982
F-16A, No. 284
Negev Squadron, IASF
Hagai Katz

F-16A-Block 10D 80-0661 No. 284—aircraft destroyed: 1 MiG-23; weapon: AIM-9L Sidewinder air-to-air missile. On 21 April 1982, an Israeli officer was killed by a land mine while he was at a southern Lebanese Army gun position in Taibe, Lebanon. The Israeli Air Force responded by attacking the Palestinian coastal town Damour. During the attack on Palestinian positions in Damour, Syrian MiG-23s attempted to engage Israeli F-16s. During the engagement Hagai Katz (in No. 284) downed one of the Floggers with an AIM-9L Sidewinder.

Netz No. 107 preparing to touch down in 2005 wearing the new tail art of Flying Wing Squadron. In 1990, the IASF became somewhat less restrictive regarding tail art and unit markings. Displayed on the nose of 107 are the six and a half kill markings obtained to date by this historic aircraft. *O. Zidon Collection*

21 April 1982
11 June 1982
F-16A, No. 107
Suffa / Gale Storm
"First Jet" Squadron, IASF
Flying Wing Squadron,
** IASF**
Ze'ef Ra
Eliezer Shkedi
Eytan Stibbe

F-16A-Block 5 78-0311 No. 107—aircraft destroyed: 4 MiG-23s; 1 Su-22; 1 SA-342L Gazelle; weapon: AIM-9L Sidewinder AAM; 20 mm M-61 Vulcan cannon. On 1 April 1982, Ze'ev Raz of the "First Jet" Squadron was the first to claim an aerial victory in F-16A Netz No. 107 when he downed a SyAAF MiG-23 Flogger. This particular jet would again go into combat on 11 June 1982, during the Lebanon War, where it would be credited with five and a half additional kills, establishing it as the leading F-16 MiG killer in the world with 6.5 kills.

On 11 June 1982, IASF pilot Eliezer Shkedi of Flying Wing Squadron claimed four aerial victories in one mission. Shkedi downed two MiG-23s, one Su-22, and one Gazelle. The Netz pilot engaged and destroyed the SyAAF aircraft with AIM-9L Sidewinders and 20 mm cannon.

In 2015, iconic F-16A No. 107 was retired from service and is now preserved and displayed at the Israeli Air and Space Force Museum at Hatzerim Air Base in the Negev Desert. The museum was established in 1977, but the museum was not open to the public until 1991.

No. 240 on the tarmac, displaying the three MiG kills acquired by Amos Mohar and Yehuda Bavli during 1982. The identity of the individual in the cockpit is unknown, but it is doubtful he is an Israeli pilot. *R. Weiss Collection*

25 May 1982
11 June 1982
F-16A, No. 240
Knights of the North
** Squadron, IASF**
Amos Mohar
Yehuda Bavli

F-16A-Block 10 78-0340 No. 240—aircraft destroyed: 2 MiG-21s; 1 Su-2; weapon: Unknown, AIM-9L Sidewinder air-to-air missile. On 25 May 1982, F-16A No. 240 was flown by Amos Mohar of the Knights of the North when he was credited with downing two Syrian MiG-21s. On 11 June 1982, Yehuda Bavli would claim a third Syrian MiG kill in F-16A No. 240. No. 240 was lost and written off on 10 April 1986.

Adorned with the Red Dragons Squadron's impressive new tail art, No. 250 waits for clearance prior to takeoff. During 1982, Netz No. 250 was assigned to the Knights of the North when it claimed two Syrian MiGs. Both Syrian jests claimed were downed with the AIM-9L Sidewinder. *O. Zidon Collection*

8 June 1982
9 June 1982
F-16A, No. 250
Knights of the North
 Squadron, IASF
Avishai Canaan
Roee Tamir

F-16A-Block 10B 78-0346 No. 250—aircraft destroyed: 1 MiG-23; 1 MiG-21; weapons: 2 AIM-9L Sidewinder missiles. On 8 June 1982, the Israeli Air Force began a bombing campaign against Syrian troop emplacements and surface-to-air missile sites in Lebanon (Operation PEACE for GALILEE). By 9 June, the Israelis would claim 25 Syrian MiGs shot down. Eleven of the kills were credited to the F-15 Baz, while fourteen aerial victories would be credited to the F-16 Netz. On 8 June, Avishai Canaan would be credited with a MiG-23 (in No. 250), and on 9 June, Roi Tamir (in No. 250) would claim a MiG-21. Both kills were made with the improved AIM-9L Sidewinder.

Triple MiG killer No. 225 is captured just prior to landing, with gear down and air brakes extended. It was lost during a training mission. *R. Weiss Collection*

8 June 1982
11 June 1982
11 June 1982
F-16A, No. 225
Knights of the North
   Squadron, IASF
Shlomo Sas
Relik Shafir

F-16A-Block 10 78-0330 No. 225—aircraft destroyed: 1 MiG-23; 2 Su-22s; 2 Sidewinder AIM-9L air-to-air missiles; 1 AIM-9P3 Sidewinder air-to-air missile. This F-16A was lost on 7 December 1986 in a training accident due to engine failure. Capt. Boaz Mehoria (No. 110 Squadron) was killed in the accident.

Now assigned to Flying Wing Squadron, F-16A No. 129 blasts into the sky. The nose of the aircraft is marked with a shared kill roundel. The shared air victory was obtained on 9 June 1982, when Eytan Stibbe and Eliezer Shkedi of "First Jet" Squadron joined forces to down a Syrian MiG-23. *O. Zidon Collection*

9 June 1982
F-16A, No. 129
"First Jet" Squadron, IASF
Eytan Stibbe

F-16A-Block 5 78-0322 No.129—aircraft destroyed: 1 MiG-23; weapon: AIM-9L Sidewinder air-to-air missile. "First Jet" Squadron F-16A No. 129 was another of the Sparrowhawks that claimed a MiG-23 Flogger on 9 June. Pilot Eytan Stibbe (in No. 129) joined the growing list of MiG killers during Operation PEACE for GALILEE, downing a Syrian MiG-23 with an AIM-9L Sidewinder missile.

Sparrowhawk No. 243 of Golden Eagle Squadron streaks across the runway at Nevatim Air Base, home of the Golden Eagles. This historic F-16A not only proved the Sparrowhawk is an agile dogfighter, but is quite capable of deep penetration bombing missions. Painted on the fuselage is the roundel for the MiG-21 kill on 9 June 1982 by Avishai Canaan. To the left a green triangle denotes 243 was one of the eight attacking F-16As during Operation OPERA. *O. Zidon Collection*

9 June 1982
F-16A, No. 243
Knights of the North
** Squadron, IASF**
Avishai Canaan

F-16A-Block 10A 78-0342 No. 243—aircraft destroyed: 1 MiG-21; weapon: AIM-9L Sidewinder air-to-air missile. On 9 June 1982, Avishai Canaan, flying with Knights of the North Squadron (in No. 243), claimed a second aerial victory during June 1982. During this engagement he destroyed a Syrian MiG-21 Fishbed with a single AIM-9L infrared all aspect missile.

F-16A No. 232 of Golden Eagle Squadron prepares to land after completing a training sortie. The Syrian roundel painted on the fuselage indicates 232 was credited with a single MiG kill during combat air operations on 9 June 1982. Golden Eagle Squadron operates single and two-seat Sparrowhawks. Many of the Sparrowhawks have been entered into the IASF upgrade program. There are no external differences between the upgraded F-16s and original aircraft; all of the avionic changes and replacements are internal. *O. Zidon Collection*

9 June 1982
F-16A, No. 232
Knights of the North
**   Squadron, IASF**
Israel (Relik) Shafir

F-16A-Block 10 78-0334 No. 232—aircraft destroyed: 1 MiG-21; weapon: AIM-9L Sidewinder air-to-air missile. During 1991, Israel (Relik) Shafir flew during the famous Operation OPERA mission. During the Lebanon War he would again distinguish himself by downing four SyAAF MiGs while flying three different Sparrowhawks. On 9 June, in No. 232 he was credited with the destruction of a MiG-21. Relik Shafir would become commander of the Israeli "Top Gun" pilot school. He would retire from the Israeli Air and Space Force (IASF) as a brigadier general.

A Mach 2.7 capable all-aspect AIM-9L Sidewinder is affixed to the wingtip of Netz No. 371. The AIM-9L (Lima) accounted for the majority of Netz aerial victories during Operation PEACE for GALILEE. The AIM-9L, with its 20 lb. warhead, was the first Sidewinder with the ability to attack from all directions, including head-on. *O. Zidon Collection*

9 June 1982
F-16A / No. 220
Knights of the North
  Squadron, IASF
Amir Nachumi

F-16A-Block 10 78-0327 No. 220—aircraft destroyed: 1 MiG-21; weapon: AIM-9L Sidewinder air-to-air missile. Amir Nachumi was the first Israeli pilot credited with an aerial victory in the F-16A (in No. 219) when on 14 July 1981 he downed a SyAAF MiG-21 with an AAM. Now a retired brigadier general, Amir Nachumi was an ace before the Lebanon War; flying the F-4E Kurnass in the Yom Kippur War he destroyed seven enemy aircraft. The general would emerge from the Lebanon War with an additional seven kills in the F-16A Sparrowhawk, giving him fourteen aerial combat victories.

On 9 June 1982, in the skies over Lebanon, he claimed a SyAAF MiG-21 (in No. 220) with an AIM-9L Sidewinder. The AIM-9L was used by Gen. Nachumi in his seven kills during Operation PEACE for GALILEE.

Netz No. 220 from Red Dragon Squadron climbs into the clear skies over Ovda Air Base in full afterburner. The MiG killer is a member of the aggressor squadron of the Red Dragons. The IASF's Red Dragon Squadron practices enemy air tactics and flies against all other IASF fighter squadrons. Red Squadron training is very similar to the USAF's Red Flag exercises. *O. Zidon Collection*

During Operation PEACE for GALILEE, F-16 No. 223 was flown by Relik Shafir on 9 June 1982, when he downed a Syrian MiG-23 with an AIM-9L. F-16A No. 223 is now deployed with Red Dragon Squadron. Here No. 223 makes a low level high speed pass over the runway at Ovda Air Base. *O. Zidon Collection*

9 June 1982
F-16A / No. 223
Knights of the North
Squadron, IASF
Relik Shafir

F-16A Block 10 78-0329 No. 223—aircraft destroyed: 1 MiG-21; weapon: AIM-9L Sidewinder air-to-air missile. On 9 June 1982, Relik Shafir claimed his first of four MiG kills in No. 223. During the engagement he locked on a MiG-23 and once all firing parameters were established he launched a heat-seeking Sidewinder missile that tracked directly to the MiG, destroying it.

A pair of Golden Eagle Squadron F-16s—No. 998 and MiG killer No. 255—are preparing for takeoff. On 9 June 1982, Netz No. 255 was operating with the Knights of the North during PEACE for GALILEE and flown by Avi Lavi when he dueled with a SyAAF MiG. Lavi destroyed the MiG with one of his AIM-9s. *O. Zidon Collection*

9 June 1982
F-16A, No. 255
Knights of the North
   Squadron, IASF
Avi Lavi

F-16A-Block 10B 78-0255 No. 255—aircraft destroyed: 1 MiG-21; weapon: AIM-9L Sidewinder air-to-air missile. On 9 June 1982, No. 255 was assigned to the Knights of the North when Avi Lavi engaged an enemy MiG-21. In the ensuing air battle Lavi was able to obtain an advantageous position over the Syrian Fishbed. Upon obtaining a good missile tone he launched a heat-seeking Sidewinder that flew true to the target, destroying the MiG.

F-16 Sparrowhawk No. 290 is another double MiG killer from the 1982 war in Lebanon. Here 29 0 proudly displays two Syrian roundels denoting the aircraft's victories. On 17 January 1995, No. 290 collided with F-16 No. 269 near Palmachim, Israel; pilot Capt. Danny Oberst did not survive the collision. The pilot of 290, identified only as "Y," did survive the midair collision. At the time of the collision both aircraft were assigned to No. 110 Squadron. *A. Dor Collection*

9 June 1982
F-16A, No. 290
Ha Negve Squadron, IASF
Pilot Unknown

F-16A-Block 10D 80-0664 No. 290—aircraft destroyed: 2 MiG-23s; weapon: AIM-9L Sidewinder air-to-air missiles.

On 10 June 1982, in the skies over Lebanon, Israeli F-16A Netz claimed thirteen aerial combat victories over Syrian MiGs. Among the victories claimed was one credited to No. 138, flown by Ami Lustig of "First Jet" Squadron. Lustig's kill was one of only five made during the second Lebanon War with the F-16's 20 mm cannon. Now assigned to Flying Wing Squadron, this historic jet climbs into a blue Israeli sky during a high speed, full afterburner launch. *O. Zidon Collection*

10 June 1982
F-16A, No. 138
"First Jet" Squadron, IASF
Ami Lustig

F-16A-Block 5 78-0325 No. 138—aircraft destroyed: 1 MiG-23; weapon: 20 mm cannon. During Operation PEACE for GALILEE, the IASF conducted a secondary operation called MOLE CRICKET 19. This operation allowed Israeli F-15 Baz and F-16 Netz pilots like Ami Lusting to roam the skies of Lebanon without fear of SAMs, during which he downed his MiG.

No. 237 taxis at an unidentified air base in Israel. As a rule, the wingtips of the F-16 are armed with live air-to-air missiles when not involved in training missions. No. 237 was lost due to an engine stall over the Negev Desert on 2 February 2000. When the pilot attempted to relight the stalled engine it caught fire, forcing the pilot to eject. *A. Dor Collection*

10 June 1982
F-16A, No. 237
Knights of the North
   Squadron, IASF
Amir Nahumi
Opher Einav

F-16A-Block 10A 78-0338 No. 237—aircraft destroyed: 2 MiG-23; 1 MiG-21; weapon: AIM-9L Sidewinder AAM. During the Lebanon War, the Syrian Air Force attempted to challenge IASF control of the skies over Lebanon and paid dearly for their efforts. On 10 June alone, IASF F-15s and F-16s destroyed eighteen SyAAF MiGs. Amir Nahumi, flying with the Knights of the North, claimed three aerial victories, downing two MiG-23s and one MiG-21 on one mission. The three kills gave Nahumi five kills as of 10 June 1982. He would go on to claim two more SyAAF MiGs on 11 June 1982, giving him seven kills in the Sparrowhawk.

No. 234 taxis to the main runway prior to launching for a training sortie and then launches from Ovda Air Base. Beside the identifying tail art 234 has been marked with three Syrian MiG kills. All three victories are credited to Amir Nachumi of Knights of the North Squadron. *O. Zidon Collection*

10 June 1982
F-16A, No. 234
Knights of the North
**   Squadron, IASF**
Amir Nachumi

F-16A-Block 10A 78-0336 No. 234—aircraft destroyed: 3 MiG-23s; weapon: 1 maneuver; 2 AIM-9 Sidewinder air-to-air missiles. On 10 June 1982, while flying No. 234, Brig. Gen. (Ret.) Nachumi downed three SyAAF MiG-23s in a single engagement: "I was on a CAP when I picked the MiGs up on radar and immediately engaged and shot down one of the MiGs." The general then pursued the other MiGs, maneuvering with them and obtaining a position to engage when his wingman yelled, "'One let me have him. Let me have him.' I did the unthinkable. I said 'have him' and pulled out, letting my wingman engage the MiGs. My wingman fired on the MiGs and failed to hit his target. I ordered him to 'break' and came in on the MiGs and destroyed two more MiG-23s."

Netz No. 111 of Flying Wing Squadron is adorned with two kill markings from the Lebanon War, as well as the green triangle that identifies No. 111 as participating in the attack on the Iraqi nuclear reactor in 1981. No. 111 demonstrates a full power takeoff using its afterburner while departing Ovda Air Base. *O. Zidon Collection*

10 June 1982
F-16A, No. 111
Yahalom / Diamond
"First Jet" Squadron, IASF
Sasha Levin

FF-16A-Block 5 78-0313 No. 111—aircraft destroyed: 1 MiG-21; 1 Gazelle; weapon: 2 AIM-9L Sidewinder air-to-air missiles.

This triple MiG killer from the Lebanon War in 1982 takes off from Ovda Air Base. No. 116 clearly shows off the sleek lines of the F-16 in the clear blue sky. Little information is available regarding the aerial victories of this Sparrowhawk. *O. Zidon Collection*

10 June 1982
F-16A, No. 116
"First Jet" Squadron, IASF
Rafi Berkovich

F-16A-Block 5 78-0137 No. 116—aircraft destroyed: 2 MiG-23s; 1 MiG-21; weapon: 2 AIM-9L Sidewinder air-to-air missiles; 1 20 mm cannon. On 10 June 1982, retired Brig. Gen. (Res) Rafi Berkovich became another Netz pilot to claim multiple MiG kills during the Lebanon War with two confirmed MiG-23s and one MiG-21. Gen. Berkovich would claim four MiGs during PEACE for GALILEE air operations in 1982.

Gen. Berkovich became instrumental in the new and upgraded F-16A/B models after 1982. After flying the newer upgrade he said, "It fits you like a glove—wherever you look the jet can take you there, anyone who flies it is impressed with the maneuvering, G-force, and aerodynamics."

Close-up of F-16A No. 118 as it taxis to takeoff. Painted on the nose of the Sparrowhawk is a Syrian roundel denoting 118's victory over a MiG-23 during air operations on 10 June 1982. F-16A No. 118 is another of the F-16s involved in Operation OPERA, flying in Eshkol flight, call sign Eshkol 03. *O. Zidon Collection*

10 June 1982
F-16A, No. 118
"First Jet" Squadron, IASF
Hagai Katz

F-16A-Block 16A 78-0318 No. 118—aircraft destroyed: 1 MiG-23; weapon: AIM-9L Sidewinder air-to-air missile. Hagai Katz would claim his second MiG on 10 June 1982, while in No. 118. His second kill—a MiG-23 Flogger—came during some of the heaviest jet vs. jet air combat since the Koran War. Katz' victory over the Flogger was accomplished with the AIM-9L Sidewinder. Approximately 38 of the F-16A Netz victories during Operation PEACE for GALILEE were with the AIM-9.

Netz No. 124 marked with a single roundel denoting a MiG-23 kill on 10 June 1982. There is little information available regarding the aerial victory. Sometime after this photograph, Negev Squadron, like other Netz Squadrons, introduced new tail art to their aircraft. No. 124 is adorned with the new tail art of Red Dragon Squadron. *O. Zidon Collection*

10 June 1982
F-16A, No. 124
Kochav / Star
"First Jet" Squadron, IASF
Shlomo Zaytman

F-16A-Block 5 78-0320 No. 124—aircraft destroyed: 1 MiG-23; weapon: 1 AIM-9L Sidewinder air-to-air missile. On 4 June 1982, F-16s from the "First Jet" Squadron took part in a mass attack against a PLO ammunition storage area in Beirut. Within two days of the attack Israel launched Operation PEACE for GALILEE and throughout June 1982, F-16s participated in CAPs. On 10 June 1982, Shlomo Zaytman (in No. 124) engaged in one of the many extensive dogfights that took place and downed a SyAAF MiG-23 with an AIM-9L Sidewinder.

11 June 1982 was the last day of continuous fighting during Operation DRUGSTORE. Just prior to the cease-fire scheduled to go into effect the afternoon of 11 June 1982, Dani Oshrat, flying with First Jet Squadron, engaged two Syrian aircraft, downing both with heat seeking air-to-air AIM-9Ls. *A. Hershko Collection*

11 June 1982
F-16A, No. 254
"First Jet" Squadron, IASF
Dani Oshrat

F-16A-Block 10B 78-0348 No. 254—aircraft destroyed: 1 MiG-21; 1 Su-22; weapon: 2 AIM-9L Sidewinder air-to-air missiles. The Israelis continued to relentlessly prosecute Operation PEACE for GALILEE with air power. Throughout the first stages of the campaign fighters and attack helicopters bombed terrorist strongholds, clearing the way for ground troops. From the very onset senior Israeli commanders knew that PEACE for GALILEE would bring the IAF in direct contact with the Syrian Air Force.

On 11 June 1982, Netz pilot Dani Oshrat of "First Jet" Squadron did indeed come in direct contact with the SyAAF and as a result engaged two Syrian aircraft (a Mig-21 and Su-22), shooting down both of them.

Sometime after 1982 this double MiG killer was reassigned to Golden Eagle Squadron, seen in two different flight configurations. In the first shot 254 flies off the wing of another F-16 over the Israel desert, while the second depicts the MiG killer just prior to landing. *O. Zidon Collection*

Netz No. 258 just moments before touching down at Nevatim Air Base, having been reassigned from Ramon Air Base in 2003. No. 258 is painted in the standard Netz color scheme and wears the tail markings of Golden Eagle Squadron. *O. Zidon Collection*

11 June 1982
F-16A, No. 258
"First Jet" Squadron, IASF
Maj. Rani Falk

F-16A-Block 10C 78-0351 No. 258—aircraft destroyed: 1 Su-22; 1 MiG-21; weapon: M-61 Vulcan 20 mm cannon. Throughout the Lebanon War, the F-16 Netz not only proved to be the primary strike aircraft for the IASF, but also a most capable MiG killer. On 11 June 1982—the last day of the war—F-16s of the IASF claimed thirteen SyAAF aircraft while engaged in air-to-ground operations. During air operations one of the "First Jet" Squadron pilots, Maj. Rafi, engaged three SyAAF MiGs. Utilizing the F-16's internal M-61A1 20 mm cannon he shot down an Su-22 and a MiG-21. Rafi is also credited with the first aerial victory ever in the F-16.

On 11 June 1982, Amos Bar was flying F-16A No. 252 when he was credited with downing a Syrian Su-22 with 20 mm cannon fire. The aerial victory of 11 June was not Bar's first kill; in fact it was number eight for the former Shahak (Mirage IIICJ) pilot. His seven prior kills were while assigned to No. 117 Squadron. The Golden Eagle Squadron now claims ownership of No. 252, where the aircraft continues to fly combat operations. *O. Zidon Collection*

11 June 1982
F-16A, No. 252
"First Jet" Squadron, IASF
Amos Bar

F-16A-Block 10B 78-0347 No. 252—aircraft destroyed: 1 Su-22; weapon: 20 mm cannon. The air battles over Lebanon during 10 and 11 June 1982 have been described by Israeli military pilots as the most intense and concentrated battles known at the time: as many as 200 jets from both sides grappled in a "box" approximately 32 × 32 miles. On one day alone the SyAAF lost 29 MiGs without a single Israeli loss. On 11 June, combat tested pilot Amos Bar of "First Jet" Squadron would claim his eighth MiG kill, downing a SyAAF Su-22 the old fashioned way with the Netz' 20 mm cannon. Prior to Operation PEACE for GALILEE Amos Bar obtained ace status with seven confirmed aerial victories.

During PEACE for GALILEE operations on 11 June 1982, Roee Tamir claimed a second aerial victory flying F-16A No. 246. Now with Golden Eagle Squadron, the MiG killer is about to touch down after a training sortie. *O. Zidon Collection*

11 June 1982
F-16A, No. 246
Knights of the North
  Squadron, IASF
Roee Tamir

F-15A-Block-10B 78-0346 No. 246—aircraft destroyed: 1 MiG-21; weapon: AIM-9L Sidewinder air-to-air missile. On 11 June 1982, while flying with Knights of the North Squadron, Roee Tamir would claim his second kill of 1982. He engaged, fired on, and destroyed a MiG-21 with a single air-to-air missile.

F-16A No. 272 in full afterburner takeoff. Markings on the nose of the fuselage indicate this aircraft has been credited with one and a half aerial combat victories. As of this writing little information is available regarding these victories. *O. Zidon Collection*

June 1982
F-16A, No. 272
"Ha Negve" Squadron/
  IASF
Moshe Rozenfeld

F-16A-Block 10C 78-0653 No. 272—aircraft destroyed: 1 MiG-21; 0.5 MiG-23; weapon: Unknown.

F-16D Block 30 Barak 1 from Valley Squadron in sand camouflage: light green and brown on top and gray on the underside. Like the F-16C, No. 364 was credited with downing a Hezbollah Ababil UAV during August 2006, but the 13 August 2006 kill was accomplished with the Rafael Python 5. The Python 5 is the newest of the Python series in IASF inventory. *O. Zidon Collection*

7 August 2006
F-16C, No. 364
Knights of the North
   Squadron, IASF
Classified

F-16C-Block 30 No. 364—aircraft destroyed: 1 Ababil Unmanned Vehicle; weapon: Python 4 air-to-air missile.

Knight of the North Squadron Barak 1 is seen standing on the tarmac, displaying a uniquely designed kill marking on its nose. The roundel depicts the national colors and emblem (cedar tree) of Lebanon, ignoring Hezbollah. On 7 August 2006, the single-seat fighter was credited with shooting down a Hezbollah Ababil UAV with a Rafael Python all aspect air-to-air missile. *O. Zidon Collection*

13 August 2006
F-16D, No. 074
Valley Squadron, IASF
Classified

F-16D-Block 30 No. 074—aircraft destroyed: 1 Ababil Unmanned Vehicle; weapon: Python 5 air-to-air missile.

One Squadron Sufa No. 844 in a graceful climb on a training sortie. It has been determined the drone downed on 6 October was an Iranian made UAV dispatched by Hezbollah on a surveillance mission into Israel. *S. Stiller Collection*

6 October 2012
F-16I, No. 844
One Squadron, IASF
Classified

F-16I-Block-30 No. 844—aircraft destroyed; unknown type unmanned aerial vehicle (UAV); weapon; Python 5 air-to-air missile. On 6 October 2012, Israeli radar units began tracking an unidentified unmanned drone operating over the Mediterranean Sea. The drone was tracked by radar when it was established it had crossed into Israeli airspace. The IASF scrambled F-16Is from One Squadron, based out of Ramon Air Base, to intercept the intruder. Once the drone was visually determined to be unarmed and on a surveillance mission the crew of F-16I No. 844 was ordered to destroy the intruder. The drone was engaged over the Negev desert, where it was destroyed by an Israeli Photon 5 air-to-air missile.

On 25 April 2013, Barak No. 340 from "First Jet" Squadron was credited with engaging and destroying an unidentified aircraft entering Israeli airspace. No. 340 is in a protective shelter and armed with air-to-air missiles, ready to engage any enemy intruders that dare attempt to cross into Israel. *O. Zidon Collection*

25 April 2013
F-16C, No. 340
"First Jet" Squadron, IASF
Classified

F-16C-Block 40 No. 340—aircraft destroyed: unknown type of unmanned aerial (UAV); weapon: air-to-air missile. On 25 April 2013, for the second time in a seven-week period the Israeli air defense system detected an unidentified aircraft attempting to enter Israeli airspace from Lebanon. All indications suggested the UAV took off from the area between Tyre and Sidon.

IASF F-16 Baraks of "First Jet" Squadron were scrambled to intercept the intruder. The UAV was acquired, deemed to be a hostile aircraft, and immediately shot down by the pilot of F-16C No. 340.

CHAPTER 10
OPERATION OPERA
7 JUNE 1981

Between 1972 and 1976, the Iraqi nuclear weapons program got underway in earnest. Its initial goal was to acquire a complete, safeguarded fuel cycle able to produce separated plutonium. For this purpose Iraq secretly signed an agreement with the French government to supply a 40MWth MTR reactor called Tammuz 1 of Osirsi.

Mossad, the Israeli intelligence service, and Israeli Defense Force Intelligence Agency had gathered intelligence regarding the potential nuclear capabilities of Iraq. The evidence clearly suggested the Iraqi nuclear program was being geared toward generating a capability to produce nuclear weapons. The intelligence gathered by Israeli agents was further corroborated in a speech on 29 October 1979 by Saddam Hussein, who proclaimed "The law of Muhammad lies in the sword, while the law of Saddam lies in the Atom." It was becoming quite evident to political and military leadership in Israel that the Tammuz 1 project (Tammuz was the Babylonian god of Hell) was a serious threat to Israel. It was decided the reactor had to be destroyed.

In 1980, months of feasibility studies and evaluation took into account everything from risk to strike force, aircraft selection, pilot selection, and countless hours of training. In February 1980, Maj. Gen. David Ivry told Defense Minister Ezer Weizman the IASF had the capability to successfully carry out an air strike against Saddam Hussein's nuclear weapons project.

The Zroa Ha'Avir Ve'Halalal (IASF) began intense training for the mission with their newly acquired F-16s. Training centered on attacking the infrastructure of the reactor and evaluating the capability of the F-16 to successfully reach the target. Simulated bombing missions with different weapon system configurations were also conducted and evaluated.

The most important element of OPERA was without a doubt the selection of the pilots tasked to carry out the mission. The eight strike pilots chosen were truly an extraordinary group of combat tested pilots with exceptional flying skills and undaunted courage. The two strike flights flew under the call signs Eshkol and Izmal, with Eshkol the first on target.

Uncharacteristically for Israel, the pilots of Eshkol and Izmal flights have been publicly identified: Ze'ev Raz (Eshkol Leader), Amos Yadlin (Eshkol 02), Dubi Yaffe (Eshkol 03), and Hagai Katz (Eshkol 04). Amir Nahumi was Izmal leader, with Yiftach Spector (Izmal 02), Relik Shafir (Izmal 03), and Ilan Ramon (Izmal 04). (Ilan Ramon would go on to be the first Israeli astronaut).

Time to Launch Operation OPERA

By the time Israel was ready to launch Operation OPERA the aircraft and pilots had been selected, all training for the mission had been completed, and all intelligence had been studied and evaluated. It was quite clear the strike package going in would be facing a high threat level.

They would be facing a vastly improved Iraqi air defense system of Russian ground-to-air SA-2, SA-3, SA-4, and SA-7 Strela missiles. They would also have to face the ever present Iraqi Air Force and their MiG fighters.

On 7 June 1982, Eshkol and Izmal flights, escorted by F-15 Baz, departed Israel for the Al-Tuwaitha site, a mere seventeen kilometers (almost ten and a half miles) south of Baghdad.

Aluf (Retired Maj. Gen.) Amos Yadlin (Eshkol 02):

> We crossed the shore, on the right, just four miles before the pull-up point. I turned on the radar and see no MiGs. Ten miles to go and Raz [Eshkol Leader] breaks radio silence: "pay attention to ground fire!"
>
> Then the chaos begins.

Flashes fill the sky, followed by little puffs of smoke. I see the reactor's silver dome. I'm at 6,500 feet and pulling 7Gs rolling over, flying inverted, gaining speed. The pipper slowly follows the trajectory line. I release the bombs and break hard and to the left, looking for missiles in the air. One zooms below and impacts with the ground. I climb in full power to rejoin the flight.

On the way the strike force flew as high as they could and were only challenged by one Iraqi MiG that closed but did not engage.

Iraqi defenses protecting the Osirak nuclear research facility on 7 June were taken totally by surprise and engaged the two (Eshkol and Izmal) attacking strike flights too late. In one minute and twenty seconds the eight F-16 Sparrowhawks destroyed the Tammuz 1 nuclear reactor.

The F-16 Netz of Operation OPERA

7 June 1981
F-16A, No. 113
"First Jet" Squadron, IASF
Lt. Col. Ze'ev Raz
(Eshkol 01)

F-16A-Block 16A 78-0315 No.113: target destroyed: Osirak Reactor: weapons: Mk 84 2,000 lb. bombs. Lt. Col. Ze'ev Raz was chosen to lead the strike aircraft during the Osirak Nuclear Reactor raid. Prior to the raid Raz flew A-4 Skyhawks (Ahit, Eagle) during the Yom Kippur War. Flying as Eshkol lead during the raid on 7 June 1981, he led Eshkol and Izmal flights through southern Jordan and headed into the Arabian Desert, passing through Saudi airspace into Iraq. After entering Iraqi airspace he descended to about a hundred feet with Eshkol and Izmal flight to prevent the strike package from exposure for the first time to Iraqi radar and SAM missile kill zones. The two flights headed directly to their pop up point at approximately 7,000 feet and with a 35 degree angle of attack began their bomb runs on the reactor.

On 7 June 1981, Lt. Col. Raz flew No. 113 during OPERA, and as mission commander was the first to attack the reactor. Here No. 113 has new tail art indicating it has been reassigned to Golden Eagle Squadron. On the nose of No. 113 is the new emblem designed especially for the attacking jets of Operation OPERA. *O. Zidon Collection*

Netz No. 107 appears in the new tail markings of Flying Wing Squadron. This iconic F-16 not only served as Amos Yadlin's aircraft during OPERA, but also is the world's leading F-16 MiG killer with 6.5 aerial victories. Netz 107 has recently been removed from service and is now in the Israeli Air and Space Force Museum. *O. Zidon Collection*

7 June 1981
F-16A, No. 107
"First Jet" Squadron, IASF
Amos Yadlin
(Eshkol 02)

F-16A-Block 5 78-0311 No. 107: target destroyed: Osirak reactor; weapons: Mk 84 2,000 lb. bombs. Sparrowhawk No. 107 is presently the leading IASF MiG killer with 6.5 kills. On 7 June 1981, No. 107 was flown by Amos Yadlin during the raid on the Iraqi nuclear reactor near Baghdad. Yadlin was flying on the wing of Lt. Col. Ze'ev Raz and followed him down the chute. Both pilots placed their 2,000 lb. bombs on target. The Mk 84s were equipped with delayed fuses and penetrators, thus ensuring explosion deep in the reactor core to maximize damage.

No. 118, which was flown by Dobbi Yaffe on 7 June 1981, has been reassigned to Golden Wing Squadron. Not only is 118 credited as one of the original attack jets in OPERA, the aircraft was also credited with an aerial victory during the Lebanon War. *O. Zidon Collection*

7 June 1981
F-16A, No. 118
"First Jet" Squadron
Dobbi Yaffe
(Eshkol 03)

F-16A-Block 16A 78-0318 No. 118: target destroyed: Osirak reactor; weapons: Mk 84 2,000 lb. bombs. The attacking Sparrowhawks were heavily loaded with two Mk 84 2,000 lb. bombs, two 370 gal. external fuel tanks under the wings, and a 300 gal. external tank on the belly of the aircraft.

No. 129 climbs into a clear blue Middle Eastern sky. The new tail art on Netz 129 indicates it is now assigned to Flying Wing Squadron. The half roundel on the nose shows No. 129 has been credited with a shared kill obtained during the Lebanon War. *O. Zidon Collection*

7 June 1981
F-16A, No. 129
"First Jet" Squadron, IASF
Hagai Katz
(Eshkol 04)

F-16A-Block 16A 78-0322 No. 129: target destroyed: Osirak reactor; weapon: Mk 84 2,000 lb. bombs. Hagai Katz (Eshkol 04) was the last of his flight to hit the Iraqi nuclear containment building. The eight attacking F-16s hit the complex at five-second intervals. Sixteen 2,000 lb. Mk 84 bombs were dropped with fourteen direct hits. IASF mission planners figured it would take eight Mk 84s to destroy the reactor.

7 June 1981
F-16A, No. 228
Knights of the North
**   Squadron, IASF**
Lt. Col. Amir Nachumi
(Izmal 01)

F-16A-Block 10 78-0332 No. 228: target destroyed: Osirak reactor; weapons: Mk 84 2,000 lb. bombs. Izmal 01 was lead aircraft in the second strike flight during the Osirak raid. F-16A No. 228 was flown by Lt. Col. Amir Nachumi, squadron leader of the Knights of the North. Nachumi was the first IASF pilot to claim a fixed-wing aerial victory in the F-16 when he downed a Syrian MiG. He is also credited with over 300 combat missions, and is one of only a few pilots in the Zroa Ha'Avir Ve'Halalal who is an acknowledged ace in two different aircraft types (F-4E and F-16).

On 7 June 1981, during the Opera raid on Saddam Hussein's nuclear reactor, Sparrowhawk No. 249 was flown by triple Ace Yiftach Spector as Izmal 02. Spector would claim ace status while flying the Mirage III and F-4 Phantom II. The lightweight fighter is depicted climbing in a full afterburner take-off. *O. Zidon Collection*

No. 249 is climbing in a full afterburner take-off. *O. Zidon Collection*

7 June 1981
F-16A, No. 249
Knights of the North
** Squadron, IASF**
Yiftach Spector
(Izmal 02)

F-16A-Block 10 78-0345 No. 249: target destroyed; Osirak reactor; weapons: Mk 84 2,000 lb. bombs. Izmal 02 was flown by retired Aluf (Maj. Gen.) Yiftach Spector, a triple ace with fifteen confirmed aerial victories. With the inclusion of pilots like Spector, Raz, and Nachumi on the OPERA mission, Israel used the elite pilots of the IASF.

Netz No. 239, flown by Relik Shafir during OPERA, in full afterburner, blasting into the skies over its home base. If you have never witnessed it, the full afterburner take-off is an impressive show of sight and sound. *O. Zidon Collection*

7 June 1981
F-16A, No. 239
Knights of the North
** Squadron, IASF**
Relik Shafir
(Izmal 03)

F-16A-Block 10A 78-0339 No. 239: target destroyed: Osirak reactor; weapons: Mk 84 2,000 lb. bombs. The eight F-16s of Eshkol and Izmal flights flew just one hundred feet off the ground during the 600 miles to Baghdad to avoid radar detection. The planning and skill of the IASF pilots was rewarded when it became obvious they had completely surprised Iraqi defenses protecting the reactor.

Often overlooked in Operation OPERA were the IASF units supporting the mission: a Grummam E-2C Hawkeye, a Boeing 707 jamming, command aircraft, tankers, and two sections of F-15s.

No. 243 from Nevatim Air Base on static display at an air show in Bino-Turnay, Czech Republic, on 4 September 2004. This is the F-16 flown by Col. Ramon during the attack on the Osirak nuclear plant. *M. Vasicek Collection*

7 June 1981
F16A, No. 243
Knights of the North
   Squadron, IASF
Ilan Ramon
(Izmal 04)

F-16A-Block 10A 78-0342 No. 243: target destroyed: Osirak reactor; weapons: Mk 84 2,000 lb. bombs. The last IASF F-16 Netz on target was No. 243 (Knights of the North) flown by Ilan Ramon. This position is without a doubt the least desirable during a bombing run. Izmal 04 was in a very hazardous position. By the time he was ingressing the target to complete his bomb run every enemy gunner knew he was coming. Even though Ramon faced the most intensive anti-aircraft fire, he was able to avoid being shot down and placed his two 2,000 lb. bombs on the dome of the reactor building.

Ilan Ramon was the least experienced IASF pilot participating in Operation OPERA. This outstanding young pilot would go on to become the first Israeli astronaut, only to be killed in the space shuttle Columbia disaster. Six years after his death Ilan Ramon's son, Assaf Ramon (21), was killed in an F-16 training mission.

Mivtza Bustan, Operation ORCHARD

The Israeli security and intelligence agency and the American Central Intelligence Agency (CIA) began monitoring an unusual amount of activity between Syria and North Korea. Three days before Operation ORCHARD was put into effect, Mossad agents documented the arrival of North Korean vessels docking at the Syrian port Tartus.

The evidence developed by the security agencies of the United States and Israel confirmed a nuclear reactor was being built in the Deir ez-Zor region of Syria. The site was being built to process plutonium and assemble a nuclear weapon using weapons grade plutonium from North Korea. When it became obvious to Israel that the United States was not going to take military action to prevent the Syrians from developing nuclear weapons capability, they took matters into their own hands.

After weeks of preparation, the Israel Air and Space Force launched Operation ORCHARD from Ramat David Air Base, Israel. On 5 September 2007, teams of elite air force Shaldag Commandos (also known as unit 5105) were secreted into the Syrian site. The Shaldag troops would be tasked with highlighting the target with laser designators.

The pilots who flew the mission were all handpicked by Commander of the Israeli Air Force Gen. Eliezer Shkedy. The pilots trained for weeks without being told what the mission involved until the night of the mission briefing.

During the evening of 5 September 2007, at least ten F-15I Ra'am armed with laser-guided bombs and eight F-16I Sufa (Storm) armed with AGM-65 Maverick missiles launched from Ramat David Air Base bound for Syria. The strike package would surely have been escorted during the mission by F-15 Baz providing CAP protection for the strike force. Electronic warfare aircraft were deployed to jam Syrian air defenses and neutralize Syrian communication and radar sites.

En route to the mysterious Syrian and North Korean complex in the Syrian Desert, the strike force attacked and destroyed a radar site in Tall al-Abuad with conventional 500 lb. bombs. As the strike package approached the site the Shaldag troops directed their laser designators at the target. The attacking aircraft released their bombs and missiles on their assigned targets. The facility was destroyed.

In May 2008, a European source reported that during Operation ORCHARD the IASF deactivated the Syrian air defense network with a secret built-in electronic warfare "kill switch" that completely rendered their system useless. Evidence suggests the IASF surely deployed their version of the American Suter airborne network attack system. The system is designed to neutralize and feed enemy radar false targeting information, and even manipulate enemy sensors. The system is very effective at attacking computers of integrated air defense systems.

"Yes We Can!" Maj. Gen. (Reserve) Eitan Ben Eliyahu stated unequivocally that Israeli military armed forces have the capability to take out Iran's nuclear weapons installations. The former commander of the Heyl Ha'Avir was quoted recently, "we have been training for it, we have the aircraft and the pilots, and we can fulfill the mission day or night in all weather conditions." Taking the general's statement at face value, many believe Operation ORCHARD was a warning to the Iranians about the IASF's true capabilities.

Knights of the North Squadron No. 250 sits heavily armed in a typical asymmetrical air-to-ground configuration with six AGM-65 Maverick missiles, much like the F-16I would have deployed during Operation ORCHARD. *O. Zidon Collection*

CHAPTER 11
F-16 FALCONS SEIZE THE SKIES

The F-16 Falcon's combat history in the Middle East has been well established by the IASF with 49 confirmed aerial victories, but a number of other countries, including the United States (6), have engaged in air-to-air combat with the Falcon: the Pakistani Air Force (10), Royal Netherlands Air Force (1), Turkish Air Force (3), and the Venezuelan Air Force (3).

Pak Fiza'iyah—Afghanistan Civil War

The Pak Fiza'iyah (Pakistani Air Force) was formed in 1947, tasked with the aerial defense of Pakistan. During the Russian invasion of Afghanistan (1979–1988), the Pakistani Air Force engaged and shot down at least eight to ten Afghan and Russian aircraft intruding into Pakistani airspace.

PAF coat of arms

17 May 1986
F-16A, No. 82723
No. 9 Squadron, PAF
Squadron Leader A.
Hameed Qadri

F-16A/B-15T-CF No. 82723—aircraft destroyed: 2 Su-22s; weapon: AIM-9P Sidewinder AAM; 20 mm guns. During a single sortie on 17 May 1986, Squadron Leader A. Hameed Qadri from No. 9 Squadron (Griffins) engaged two Russian Sukhois Su-22s while flying in F-16 No. 82723.

The squadron leader was engaged in a CAP over Parachinar when he engaged the two Su-22s. Qadri downed the first of his two kills with an AIM-9P Sidewinder and the second with the F-16's 20 mm cannon. Unfortunately, Flight Leader Qadri lost his life in a crash in 2002.

Pakistani Air Force F-16 No. 85723 is credited with destroying an Su-22 on 1 May 1986. This computer generated artwork depicts the Afghani Su-22 after being hit by an AIM-9L Sidewinder launched by Squadron Leader Hameed Qadri. F-16 No. 85723 is credited with the first aerial victory for a Falcon in the PAF. The aircraft was on a night training mission and while returning to Kamra Air Base suffered engine failure, forcing Squadron Leader Syed Hassan Raza to eject. *Digital Artwork by Najam Khan*

30 March 1987
F-16A, No. 82701 (?)
No. 9 Squadron, PAF
Wing Commander Abdul Razzak

F-16A/B Block 15 No. 82701 (?)—aircraft destroyed: 1 AN-26; weapon: AIM-9 AAM. Wing Commander Abdul Razzak launched from the Pakistani air base at Minhas Kamra on 30 March 1987 to intercept a Russian/Afghani aircraft suspected to be involved with an electronic intelligence mission. During the successful interception the aircraft was identified as an AN-26. Wing Commander Razzak downed the AN-26 with a single AIM-9P Sidewinder. Abdul Razzak would rise to air vice marshal before his tragic death in a crash on 20 February 2003.

16 April 1987
F-16A, No. 85722
No. 14 Squadron, PAF
Flight Lt. Badar-ul-Islam

F-16A/B Block 15 No. 85722—aircraft destroyed: Su-22; weapon: AIM-9 Sidewinder AAM. On 16 April 1987, Flight Lt. Badar-ul-Islam from No. 14 Squadron (The Tail Choppers) was vectored to intercept two Su-22 Fitters intruding into Pakistani airspace near Thael. As he approached the Sukhois Su-22s they attempted to evade the PAF F-16, but Islam was able to close on the intruders and within seconds launched an air-to-air missile that quickly destroyed the first Fitter.

The flight lieutenant was ordered to break away as he approached the Afghanistan border, but he did manage to get off a second missile. When he looked back he saw a large flash where the second Fitter was last seen. The PAF awarded him credit for one kill on 16 April 1987.

F-16A No. 85722 on final approach to Kong AFB, Turkey, during the Anatolian Eagle 2012 air exercise. On 16 April 1987, the aircraft was assigned to No. 14 Squadron when Squadron Leader Badar engaged and destroyed an Afghan Su-22. *K. Daws Collection*

4 August 1988
F-16A, No. 85725
No. 14 Squadron, PAF
Squadron Leader Athar Imam Bokhari

F-16A–Block 15 81-0923 No. 85725—aircraft destroyed: 1 Su-25; weapon: 1 AIM-9P Sidewinder AAM. The Sukhoi Su-25 Frogfoot is a single-seat, twin-engine jet aircraft designed and built for close air support for ground troops.

On 4 August 1988, Squadron Leader Athar Bokhari was scrambled from Kamra, Pakistan, to intercept four unidentified radar contacts. The radar contacts were positively identified as Su-25s. Bokhari obtained a radar lock on one of the intruders and armed a Sidewinder. The missile's infrared seeker head began tracking its target. At approximately seven nautical miles—well within Pakistani airspace—the Su-25 turned in front of Bokhari. At three nautical miles he launched his starboard AIM-9L Sidewinder and within seconds he observed a large fireball.

The pilot of the stricken Frogfoot was able to eject and was subsequently captured, whereupon it was established he was Col. Alexandrov of the Soviet Armed Forces.

PAF F-16 No. 85725 claimed a Russian Su-25 on 4 August 1988 with Flight Leader Bokhari at the controls. The Su-25 was destroyed with an AIM-9L short range, all aspect Sidewinder. F-16 No. 85725 is in full afterburner after downing the Su-25 and preparing to engage four other bandits that entered Pakistani air space. *Digital Artwork by Najam Kahn*

3 November 1988
31 January 1989
F-16A, No. 85728, 84717, 85711
No. 9 Squadron, PAF
Flight Lt. Khalid Mahmoud

F-16A/B–Block 15 Nos. 85728, 85717, and 85711—aircraft destroyed: 2 MiG-23MDLs; 1 Su-22; 1 AN-24; weapons: 4 AIM-9P Sidewinder AAMs. Pakistani Air Force Flight Lt. Khalid Mahmoud (No. 14 Squadron) has been credited with the downing of four enemy aircraft that intruded into Pakistani airspace.

On 12 September 1988, while flying F-16 tail number 85728, the flight lieutenant scrambled from Kamra and was vectored to intercept MiG-23 MLDs over Nawagai. During the engagement Mahmoud successfully destroyed two Floggers with AIM-9 Sidewinders.

During November 1988 and on January 1999, Flight Lt. Mahmoud would again engage enemy aircraft: on 3 November 1988 he engaged and destroyed an Su-22, and on 31 January 1999 he destroyed an An-24.

Squadron Leader Khaild Mahmood's first aerial victory while flying F-16A No. 85728 on 12 September 1988 was confirmed. Here the Pak Fiza'iyah (Pakistani Air Force) F-16A was captured after landing. At the time the photograph was taken F-16 No. 85728 was participating in air operations during Anatolian Eagle 2012 in Kong, Turkey. *K. Daws Collection*

Pakistani Air Force Air Chief Marshal Tahir Rafique Butt about to enter the cockpit of No. 85711. This F-16 was flown by Flight Leader Khalid Mahmood when he shot down a Soviet An-24. The date and location of this photograph are unknown. *N. Kahn-pafwallpaper*

On 3 November 1988, F-16A No. 84717 was assigned to 9 Squadron when Flight Leader Mahmood downed an Afghan Su-22 Fitter. Here the Afghan fighter is engulfed in flames just prior to crashing. *Digital Artwork by Najam Khan*

20 November 1988
F-16A, Unknown
No. 14 Squadron, PAF
Flight Lt. Muhammad
   Abbas Khattak

F/16A/B-Block 15 (Unknown)—aircraft destroyed: 1 AN-26; weapon: AIM-9 AAM. On 20 November 1988, an F-16 from No. 14 Squadron piloted by Flight Lt. Khattak engaged a Soviet An-26 on a recce mission inside Pakistani airspace. The Soviet An-26 was destroyed with an AIM-9. Khattak would later become chief of the air staff, PAF (1994–1997).

7 June 2002
F-16B, 83605
No. 9 Squadron, PAF
Squadron Leader Zulfiqar Ayub
Squadron Leader Afzal Aman

F-16B-Block 15 No. 83605—aircraft destroyed: Searcher II UAV; weapon: AIM-9L AAM. Pakistani Air Force F-16Bs were received under the Peace Gate III program from the United States.

On 7 June 2002, Squadron Leaders Zulfiqar Ayub and Afzal Aman (No. 9 Multirole Fighter Squadron) intercepted an Indian Air Force Searcher II UAV near Lahore. In the brief engagement, the crew of 83605 locked on to the UAV and launched an AIM-9L Sidewinder. The wreckage of the destroyed UAV fell off at Dogran Kalan Village, southwest of Lahore.

F-16B 83605 was flown by Squadron Leaders Ayub and Aman when they shot down an Indian Search II UAV with an AIM-9 Sidewinder. Evidence suggests the UAV was a Chinese DJI Phantom 3. Little information regarding the photograph of 83605 is available. *N. Khan-pafwallpaper*

Fuerza Aerea Venezolana (Venezuela) F-16 Aerial Victory

During 1982–1983, the Venezuelan Air Force purchased 24 F-16A/B Falcons under the Peace Delta program from the United States. For a time Venezuela was the only Latin American country to have received and deployed the Falcon. The F-16s of the Venezuelan Air Force are assigned to *Escuadron* 161 (Caribes) and *Escuadron* 162 (Gavilanes) operating with Fighter Air Group 16 from El Libertador Air Base.

On 27 November 1992, the Venezuelan military launched a failed coup attempt against President of Venezuela Carlos Andres Perez. During the coup a small number of air force F-16 pilots remained loyal to the government. Two F-16 pilots—Lt. Beltran Vielma and Capt. Helimenas Labarca—who remained loyal to the Perez government were able to get two F-16s airborne that were on alert at El Libertador Air Base.

Lt. Vielma is credited with shooting down two OV-10 Broncos commandeered by the rebels and deployed against Venezuelan military troops. The first Bronco was successfully engaged and shot down with a Sidewinder AIM-9P, while the second kill was accomplished with the Falcon's 20 mm cannon. Capt. Labarca was credited with shooting down a single AT-27 Tucano.

F-16s also attacked and destroyed 8 F-5 Freedom Fighters on the ground at Barquisimeto Air Base.

27 November 1992
F-16A/B, No. 4226 (?)
Squadron 161, FAV
Lt. Beltran Vielma

F-16A/B-Block 15 No. 84-1351 / 4226 (?)—aircraft destroyed: 2 OV-10 Broncos; weapon: AIM-9P AAM, 20 mm cannon.

27 November 1992
F-16A/B, No. Unknown
Squadron 161, FAV
Capt. Helimenas Labarca

F-16A/B-Block 15 No. Unknown—aircraft destroyed: AT-27 Tucano; weapon: AIM-9P AAM (?).

27 December 1992
F-16D No. 90-0778
33rd TFS, 363rd TFW
Capt. Gary L. "Nordo"
North
(Benji 41)

F-16C-GD-42H 90-0778—aircraft destroyed: MiG-25; weapon: AIM-120 Slammer; Tail Code: SW.... On 5 April 1991, the United Nations Security Council passed resolution 688, barring all Iraqi fixed and rotary wing aircraft from airspace south of the 33rd parallel.

Air operations conducted by Saddam Hussein's air force during '91–'92 demonstrated he had no intention of complying with resolution 688. Right from the very end of the 1991 Gulf War until the invasion of Iraq in 2003, there were countless military engagements between coalition forces and Iraqi command and control systems, AAA sites, radar sites, and surface-to-air missile sites. One of the most noted clashes took place on 27 December 1992, when an Iraqi MiG-25 aircraft violated the no fly zone and entered airspace south of the 33rd parallel.

At approximately 10:42 a.m. local time on Sunday, 27 December 1992, Capt. Gary North, flying as Benji 41, and his wingman were alerted by an E-3 AWACS that Iraqi MiG-25s had entered the no fly zone.

Capt. North was flying F-16D No. 90-0778, armed for an air-to-air mission with two AIM-120 AMRAAM and two AIM-9M Sidewinders when he was tasked to intercept the Iraqi Foxbats.

On 28 October 1998, Col. Paul "PK" White interviewed Capt. North for an article he authored, "Nordos' MiG Kill." In the article Capt. North described the moment of missile impact: "I saw three separate detonations, the nose and left wing broke apart instantly, and the tail section continued into the main body of the jet, and finally one huge fireball."

On 27 December 1992, Capt. Gary L. North was flying this F-16 when he became the first USAF pilot to down an enemy aircraft in the F-16 Falcon. Capt. North's MiG-25 kill on 27 December was also the first kill with the AIM-120A. Here Col. North is at the controls in February 1993 as he departs Shaw AFB. *D. Brown Collection*

First F-16 AIM-120 Kill (AMRAAM)

The 27 December 1992 MiG-25 Foxbat kill of Capt. Gary L. North of the 33rd TFS/363rd TFW from Shaw AFB, South Carolina, accomplished two firsts for the USAF.

F-16D No. 90-0778 was the first American Viper (Falcon) to be credited with an aerial victory in air-to-air combat. The downing of the Iraqi MiG-25 by Capt. North was also the first time $500,000 AMRAAM (AIM-120) was used in combat. North locked up the MiG-25 at approximately three nautical miles and launched the weapon, which guided to impact and totally destroyed the Russian built Foxbat.

An F-16C assigned to the 23rd Fighter Squadron taxiing to the flight line during Operation NORTHERN WATCH. Attached to the aircraft's wingtip is an AIM-120A. The AIM-120A missile is capable of all-weather day and night operations. Completing the weapons load are the AIM-9P Sidewinder and AGM-88 high speed anti-radiation missile (HARM). *TSgt. K.J. Gruenwald, USAF*

17 January 1993
F-16C, No. 86-0262
23rd FS, 52nd FW
Lt. Craig D. "Trigger"
    Stevenson
(Devil 01)

F-16C-GD-30D 86-0262—aircraft destroyed: MiG-23; weapon: AIM-120 Slammer; Tail Code: SP. In April 1991, Operation PROVIDE COMFORT was instituted to defend the Kurds north of the 36th parallel because of the continued disregard by the Iraqi government of the mandates set forth in resolution 688.

On the second anniversary of the Gulf War, the Iraqi Air Force challenged American aircraft enforcing the no fly zone, and in so doing paid the ultimate price for their indiscretion.

Four American F-16s operating from Incirlik Air Base, Turkey (call sign Devil flight), were on patrol when Devil 01—Lt. Craig D. "Trigger" Stevenson—made radar contact with Iraqi aircraft launching from an airfield south of the 36th parallel. Codenamed Caddy, the airfield had often been the site from which enemy aircraft launched to attack Kurdish targets. The Iraqi MiG-23s picked up on radar by "Trigger" Stevenson had taken off and were heading toward Devil flight. At the time of original contact they were approximately thirty nautical miles away and moving fast. Devil lead and his wingman cleaned off (jettisoned two 370 gal. fuel tanks) their aircraft and readied themselves for battle. The MiG pilot was climbing toward Devil flight like a bat out of hell and in no time had crossed into the no fly zone. Lt. Stevenson was cleared by the E-3 AWACS controller to kill the intruder.

While maneuvering his aircraft into an offensive position the MiG pilot made a hard left turn to engage Stevenson, placing the MiG pilot in maximum range of Stevenson's AIM-120s. With a lock established on the MiG, Devil lead launched an AIM-120 from his left wing tip. Imagine his utter surprise when the missile failed to fire. Without hesitation Lt. Stevenson armed and fired the AIM-120 on his right wing; the missile guided directly into the Flogger, which was still heading directly at Devil flight. After detonation the MiG was seen to descend in a huge fireball. The pilot was not seen to eject and it is assumed he went down with the MiG.

No. 86-0262 sits on the ramp of the 52nd Fighter Wing of the Ohio Air National Guard. Although not marked in this photograph as a MiG killer, it is surely the jet flown by Trigger Stevenson on 17 January 1993 when he downed his MiG-23 Flogger with a single AIM-120A (Slammer). *P. Martin Collection*

Balkans 1994–1995 and 1999

On 12 April 1993, the United Nations Security Council passed resolution 781, establishing protection for NATO troops deployed in the Balkans. In part, Security Council resolution 781 set up a no fly zone over Bosnia-Herzegovina. Enforcement of the resolution would be carried out by NATO aircraft from the United States, Netherlands, and France operating from air bases in Italy and aircraft carriers in the Adriatic.

By the end of December 1994, NATO aircraft operating in support of Operation DENY FLIGHT would fly over 47,000 sorties. During 1994 and again in 1995, two incidents would emerge from Operation DENY FLIGHT that captured the interest of the American public: the Banja Luka incident 28 February 1994, and the incident at Mrkonjic' Grad 2 June 1995.

Regarding the Banja Luka incident on 28 February 1994, six Republika Srpska Air Force J-21 Jastreb attack aircraft were discovered while on a bombing mission against the Bratstvo military factory. After repeated warnings by NATO aircraft they continued their attack. Failing to heed warnings, United States Air Force F-16s operating in concert with NATO air force units engaged the J-21 light attack aircraft and four of the JastrebS were shot down by two American F-16s.

The second incident took place on 2 June 1995, in the skies over Mrkonjic' Grad, when Bosnian Serb Army units downed an American F-16 with an SA-6 Gainful surface-to-air missile. The F-16 (Basher 52) was flown by young USAF Capt. Scott "Zulu" O'Grady, who safely ejected from his stricken aircraft. The captain was rescued on 8 June 1995.

The following is a brief account of the air battle of Black and Knight Flight on 28 February 1994, when they downed four J-21s.

28 February 1994
F-16C, No. 89-2137
F-16C, No. 89-2009
526th FS, 86th FW
Capt. Robert G. Wright
(Black 03)
Capt. Steve L. "Yogi" Allen
(Knight 25)

F-16C-GD-40 89-2137
F-16C-GD-40E 89-2009—aircraft destroyed: 4 J-21s; weapon: 1 AIM-120 Slammer, 3 AIM-9M Sidewinders; Tail Code: AV. On 28 February 1993, a small armada of six Soko J-21 Galeb/Jastreb and two Soko J-22 Orao of the Serbian Air Force were detected by NATO Airborne Early Warning aircraft (NAEW) while engaged in a bombing mission against a Bosnian Muslim munitions factory near the town Novi Tranvink, in clear violation of the no fly zone.

Two flights of F-16s (call signs Black and Knight from the 526th FS, flying out of Aviano, Italy) were alerted by NATO early warning aircraft. Black 03 Capt. Robert G. Wright and his wingman, Capt. Scott F. O'Grady (Black 04), were tasked with intercepting the J-21s.

After completing their bombing mission the Serbian jets beat a hasty retreat from the area. The two J-22s managed to make it safely back to their base at Udbina; after a number of warnings by Black flight, Black flight was cleared to engage the six fleeing J-21s. The first J-21 was shot down by Capt. Wright, who bagged the enemy aircraft with an AIM-120. The remaining J-21s attempted to evade Wright's attack by maneuvering their aircraft down on the deck and making a run for it. Capt. Wright was able to continue his pursuit of the J-21s until he was in range to strike with his AIM-9M Sidewinders. After establishing a good tone with the AIM-9s he pulled the trigger and launched the missiles; both found their mark and two more J-21s were killed.

After downing the three enemy aircraft Capt. Wright was nearly out of fuel and turned the air battle over to his wingman, Capt. O'Grady. O'Grady had been flying cover for Black 03 during his battle with the Serbian jets. Capt. O'Grady, like Wright, was low on fuel, but maneuvered his aircraft into position to engage one of the enemy aircraft. He armed and launched one of his AIM-9 Sidewinders at the remaining Galeb/Jastreb. Initial evidence suggested the missile failed to lock on to the target. Capt. O'Grady had to disengage because of bingo fuel status and rejoined with Capt. Wright. Once they reestablished contact they headed out over the Adriatic to refuel from an orbiting KC-135 tanker.

After Black flight departed the area the AWACS controller contacted Knight Flight and vectored Capt. Steve L. Allen and his wingman to intercept what was left of the J-21s. Capt. Allen managed to maneuver his aircraft into position to get off a Sidewinder that tracked directly to a J-21 before it had a chance to cross the international border. The Sidewinder destroyed the enemy aircraft.

The two F-16CG Night Falcons credited with the shoot down of four J-21s on 28 February 1994 are profiled in this series of photographs. The first photograph of F-16CG No. 89-2137 was at the Malta International Air Show in 2002 while on static display with other F-16s. The tail markings identify the F-16CG as assigned to a NATO air base in Italy. *Ricardo Aysa Calahorra Collection*

F-16C No. 89-2009 on the ramp at Moody AFB. Ground crews provide maintenance prior to takeoff. The second outstanding shot of 2009 was taken while engaged in a full afterburner takeoff while assigned to the European Air Command. *P. Martin Collection*

Aftermath of Banja Luka

The United States Air Force and NATO only recognize four Serbian J-21 Galeb/Jastreb downed on 28 February 1994 by F-16 pilots of the 526th FS Black Knights. Capt. Robert G. Wright was credited with three confirmed kills, while Capt. Steve L. Allen was credited with one confirmed kill.

An unnamed Yugoslav pilot reported all six of the light attack J-21s went down that day. A total of five were shot down with three pilots killed in action: Capt. 1st Class Ranko Vukmirovic (KIA), Capt. 1st Class Zvezdan Pesic (KIA), and Capt. 1st Class Goran Zaic (KIA) have all been identified as lost on 28 February 1994. Maj. Uros Studen and Capt. 1st Class Zlatko Mikerevic ejected from their damaged aircraft and were rescued. Capt. 1st Class Zlatan Crnalic' landed his heavily damaged aircraft. Both Crnalic' and his aircraft survived the air engagement to fly another day.

The events of 28 February 1994 were only a prelude of what was to come in the Balkans in 1999.

NATO at War—Kosovo 1999

During 1999, Yugoslav President Slobodan Milosevic was employing his military and security force to depopulate and destroy the Albanian majority in Kosovo. On 24 March 1999, the entire membership of NATO interceded in the Balkans, launching Operation ALLIED FORCE to ensure the withdrawal of all Yugoslavian military, police, and other forces from Kosovo.

The military objective of NATO was to destroy, degrade, or damage air defenses and high value military targets, as well as dual purpose infrastructure in Yugoslavia and Kosovo. NATO planned to accomplish their military objectives with the exclusive use of air power, deploying over 1,000 aircraft to take on the armed forces of Slobodan Milosevic, which were substantial. The ground force of the Yugoslavian army numbered over 114,000. The air defense force possessed over 1,800 anti-aircraft artillery weapons, along with a mixture of over 100 surface-to-air missile systems (SA-2; SA-3; SA-6, 7, and 9; SA-13; SA-14; and SA-16). At the time of Operation ALLIED FORCE the Yugoslavian Air Force was comprised of over 240 combat aircraft, including MiG-21s and MiG-29s.

From the inception of Operation ALLIED FORCE on 24 March 1999, to the agreement with the Milosevic government to withdraw from Kosovo on 20 June 1999, NATO air forces flew over 38,000 combat missions in support of ALLIED FORCE. During air operations NATO lost only two aircraft: an F-117 Nighthawk and an F-16 Falcon. Both pilots were rescued. During air operations NATO forces destroyed six Yugoslav Air Force MiG-29s.

This historic Falcon is in a far more relaxed setting than on 5 April 1999, when Lt. Col. Geczy claimed the last aerial victory of Operation ALLIED FORCE. 91-0353 is parked on the line next to an F-15 Eagle at the Amigo Air Show in El Paso, Texas, on 23 October 2004. *A. Morrell*

5 April 1999
F-16CJ, No. 91-0353
77th TS, 20th FW
Lt. Col. Michael H. Geczy
(Dog 01)

F-16CJ-GD-50C 91-0353—aircraft destroyed: MiG-29; weapon: AIM-120B Slammer; Tail Code: SW. During a combat mission on 5 April 1999, Lt. Col. Geczy's flight was en route to a midair refueling with an Air Force tanker when the AWACS controller broadcasted a MiG warning.

Lt. Col. Geczy and his flight immediately began to maneuver, placing their flight into an advantageous position. Working with the E-3 AWACS, Lt. Col. Geczy was able to locate the enemy MiG over Valjevo and arm and launch one of his AIM-120s, which upon impact totally destroyed the Serbian MiG. The pilot of the Serbian aircraft was identified as Lt. Col. Milenko Pavlovic, who was killed. Lt. Col. Pavlovic was the commander of the Knights Squadron at the time of his death.

Royal Netherlands Air Force (Koninklijke Luchtmach [Klu])

24 March 1999
F-16AM, No. J-063
322nd Squadron, RNLAF
Capt. Peter Tankink
(Unknown)

F-16AM-15AC OCU - 86-003 (J-063)—aircraft destroyed: MiG-29; weapon: AIM-120 Slammer; Tail Code: (?). For the first time since WWII, the Royal Netherlands Air Force (RNLAF) claimed an aerial victory during Operation ALLIED FORCE. On the night of 24 March 1999, four Dutch F-16AMs were engaged in a CAP when informed by an AWACS controller that three MiG-29s had just launched from an air base near Belgrade. The flight of four Dutch F-16AMs led by Capt. Peter Tankink immediately headed toward the threat. Once Capt. Tankink picked up the threat on radar he launched a single AIM-120 (AMRAAM). Within thirty seconds Tankink's missile struck the MiG-29, destroying it in a firery explosion. The MiG pilot, identified as Lt. Col. Milutinovic, was able to safely eject.

Capt. Peter Tankink was flying J063 on 24 March 1999 when he claimed the first aerial victory for a Dutch pilot since WWII. F-16 J-063 is painted in the anniversary markings of the 322nd Polly Parrot Squadron at Leeuwarden Air Base, Netherlands, on 28 August 2005. J-063 prepares to launch from Leeuwarden with two other F-16s from the 322nd. If you look just below the canopy you can clearly see the black silhouette of a MiG-29 in recognition of the Tankink victory. *R. Wilthof Collection*

J-063 with landing gear still extended, appearing to have just launched from Leeuwarden Air Base armed with AIM-120s. *R. Wilthof Collection*

Turkish Air Force (Turk Hava Kuvvetleri)

On 22 June 2012, strained relations between Ankara and Damascus reached critical mass when Syrian air defense units shot down a Turkish Air Force RF-4E Phantom II on a reconnaissance mission. The Turkish aircraft disappeared over the Mediterranean Sea approximately eight miles from the Syrian town Latakia. Rumors claimed the Phantom was shot down with a Russian SA-5 Gammon (S-200) long range mobile surface-to-air missile.

The 22 June 2012 incident clearly worsened already strained relations between the neighboring countries. The antagonistic relationship between Turkey and Syria would only worsen with the deployment of Russian troops and combat aircraft into Syria.

Saber Rattling Turns Deadly
One could only expect the downing of the Russian Su-24 Fencer on 24 November 2015 would ratchet up already existing tensions between Turkey and Russia along the Syrian border. As early as 15 September 2015, Russian MiG-29s intruded into Turkish airspace, targeting TuAF F-16s. The MiG-29s engaged the F-16s for approximately five minutes with their weapon system fire control radar. On 3 and 4 October 2015, Russian aircraft (Su-30M and Su-24s) again intruded into Turkish airspace, targeting Turkish warplanes.

Russian combat aircraft, including the Su-24 Fencer shot down on 24 November, were deliberately violating the sovereign airspace of NATO member Turkey. Russia had been testing NATO nations all over the world with constant intrusions into NATO airspace with Tu-95 Bear and Tu-160 Blackjack bombers.

16 September 2013 **F-16C, No. 92-0005** **182 Filo (Squadron), TuAF** **Classified**	F-16C-Block 40H 92-0005—aircraft destroyed: Mi-17 Hip-H Helicopter; weapon AIM-9 AAM. On 16 September 2013, Turk Hava Kuvvetleri (TuAF) acknowledged an F-16 Falcon from 182 Filo had intercepted and destroyed a Syrian single rotor, medium twin turbine transport Mi-17 Hip multi-role helicopter. The engagement took place near the border of the two countries.

Turk Hava Kuvvetleri (Turkish Air Force) F-16 Night Falcon No. 92-0005 belongs to the 182 Filo and was at Konya, Turkey, on 7 May 2015. Clearly visible on the fuselage under the canopy is the silhouette of a Syrian Mi-17 Hip helicopter shot down on 16 September 2013. *R. Bergmann Collection*

During 4–15 May 2015, over 100 fighters from eleven countries participated in NATO Tiger Meet 2015 exercises at Konya Air Base, Turkey. Among the aircraft at Tiger Meet 2015 was Turkish Air Force F-16 No. 91-0008, credited with the destruction of a Syrian Air Force MiG-23 Flogger on 23 March 2014, here off the wing of a KC-135 Stratotanker. *Turkish Air Force*

23 March 2014
F-16C, No. 91-0008
182 Filo (Squadron), TuAF
Clasified

F-16C- Block 40H 91-0008—aircraft destroyed: MiG-23MB; weapon: AIM-120 AMRAAM. On 23 March 2014, F-16s from 182 Filo (Squadron) scrambled from Diyarbakir Air Base to investigate an intrusion into Turkish airspace. The intruders were identified as MiG-23MB Floggers. The Mikoyan-Gurevich MiG-23 pilots were warned four times to alter their course before entering over southern Turkey. One of the Flogger pilots turned back to Syria, while the second pilot continued into Turkish airspace. The Syrian intruder was destroyed by an AIM-120 AMRAAM fired from F-16 tail number 91-0008. The MiG-23 fell in the vicinity of Kesab, on the Syrian side of the border.

16 May 2015
F-16C, No. Unknown
Squadron Unknown
Classified

F-16A–Block 40H No. Unknown—aircraft destroyed: helicopter / surveillance drone; weapon: air-to-air missile. On 16 May 2015, two Turkish F-16s scrambled from Incirlik Air Base in southern Turkey. Turkish air defense radar units in southern Turkey had detected an airborne threat entering Turkish airspace from Syria.

The intruder was identified by the Turkish Air Force as a Syrian helicopter that was quickly engaged in the area of the Cilvegozu border crossing in the Hatay region of southern Turkey. Syria countered the Turkish claim by identifying the aircraft as a small surveillance drone instead of a helicopter.

16 October 2015
F-16C, No. Unknown
182 Filo (Squadron) TuAF
Classified

F-16C- Block H—Tail No. Unknown—aircraft destroyed: Russian Orlan-10 Drone; weapon: AIM-9 Sidewinder air-to-air missile. On 21 September 2015, Russia, in an attempt to shore up the regime of President Bashar al-Assad, began the deployment of Russian combat air power to an airfield in the western province of Lalakia, Syria.

The initial deployment of combat air power consisted of approximately 12 Sukhoi Su-24M Fencer long-range all-weather strike bombers, 12 Sukhoi Su-25 Frogfoot ground attack aircraft, and 4 Sukhoi Su-27 Flanker multi-role air superiority fighters. The fixed wing Russian air assets were augmented with transport and attack helicopters.

Sources in Turkish and United States intelligence agencies have confirmed that included in the deployment of combat aircraft were a variety of UAVs.

On or about 30 September 2015, Russian combat aircraft began conducting air strikes in Syria near its border with Turkey. During the first week of October 2015, Russian aircraft began harassing Turkish aircraft operating within their own national airspace. On 3 and 4 October 2015, two separate intrusions into Turkish airspace were reported by the Turkish general staff in Ankara. During the first violation on 3 October, a Russian Sukhoi Su-30SM Flanker-C had gone as far as locking on to Turkish F-16s with its weapon systems tracking radar. A similar incident took place on 6 October, when a MiG-29 Fulcrum violated Turkish airspace and again locked on to Turkish F-16s operating in their own airspace.

After numerous warnings to the Russians and Syrians, the intrusions into Turkish airspace continued unabated. On 16 October 2015, Turkish Air Force radar units detected yet another intruder into their airspace. After three warnings went unheeded, Turkish F-16s from 182 Filo (Squadron) operating from Diyarbakir Air Base located the intruder approximately two miles inside Turkish airspace. After failing to respond to warnings the aircraft was engaged by the F-16s. In all probability the intruder was shot down with an AIM-9.

The wreckage of a UAV was discovered near the village Deliosman in Kilis province, Turkey. Preliminary examination of the wreckage tentatively identified the UAV as being similar to a Russian made Orlan-10 reconnaissance drone.

Tension in the airspace along the Turkish and Syrian border continues to escalate as the number of combat aircraft from the American led coalition, Turkish Air Force, Syrian Air Force, and Russian Air Force continue air operations over Syria and Iraq against ISIS.

On 16 October 2015, Turkish Air Force F-16s of 182 Filo shot down a UAV near the border with Syria; here is the wreckage of the UAV recovered by Turkish troops, which appears to be similar to a modified Russian Orlan-10 reconnaissance aircraft. *Turkish Government Public Release*

Sukhoi Su-24 Fencer RED 54—seen at the International Mask Airshow outside Moscow in 2007—is identical to the Su-24 supersonic all-weather, variable sweep wing, twin-engine bomber shot down by F-16s from 182 Filo of the Turkish Air Force on 24 November 2015. *O. Zidon Collection*

24 November 2015
F-16C, No. Unknown
182 Filo (Squadron), TuAF
Classified

F-16C- Block H–Tail No. Unknown—aircraft destroyed: Sukhoi Su-24M2; weapon: AIM-120C7 air-to-air missile. On 24 November 2015, escalated tensions along the Turkey/Syria border erupted when Turkish Air Force F-16s from 182 Filo intercepted two Russian Sukhoi Su-24 Fencers in Turkish airspace. The Turkish general staff in Ankara reported that their F-16s offered repeated warnings (ten within five minutes) that the intruding Russian aircraft were in Turkish airspace and ordered the Russian aircraft to immediately turn and head south. The report continued, stating that one of the Russian pilots immediately headed south, leaving Turkish airspace. The second Su-24 remained in Turkish airspace, whereupon it was engaged, fired on, and destroyed by an AIM-120C7. The downing of the Sukhoi Su-24 is the first confirmed aerial victory for the new AIM-120C7.

The two crewmen—identified as Lt. Col. Oleg Peshkov (pilot) and Capt. Konstantin V. Murakhtin (copilot)—were seen ejecting from the burning Fencer, and as they descended in their parachutes they were subjected to ground fire. Reports indicate Lt. Col. Peshkov was killed as a result of ground fire. His copilot reached the ground safely and was rescued.

CHAPTER 12
BATTLE FOR THE SKIES

Aerial Combat (Dogfight)

Over a hundred years have passed since aerial battles (dogfights) were first conducted during WWI. Even after thirty years without a single dogfight, the IASF continues to prepare for such a scenario. Like their counterparts in the IASF, the USAF continues air-to-air and air-to-ground training (Red Flag—Top Gun) unabated. Today's F-15 Eagle and F-16 Falcon represent a quantum leap in their capabilities from the original designs in the 1960s. With continued upgrading to avionics and weaponry the service life of these iconic aircraft will be dramatically extended. For example, the USAF will keep approximately 170 Eagles in service through 2025. Like the Americans, the Israelis have continuously upgraded the F-15 Baz and today, the Baz 2000 may appear similar to Baz of past decades, but when it comes to deadliness and adaptability it is an entirely different beast. The only thing more potent today than the F-15 Eagle is the Lockheed Martin F-22 Raptor. The Raptor, with its full aspect stealth capability to counter air defense systems, supercruise capability, and Mach 2 (1,522 mph) speed make it the most lethal aircraft flying today.

Air Force F-15E Strike Eagle tail number 90-0241 of the 142nd Fighter Wing, Oregon Air National Guard in 2006, while participating in a world mission. The Strike Eagle has updated electronics and long-range infra-red search and track sensors. *Cleared for release by the USAF, T. Miller Collection*

The F-22 Raptor is at the moment the only deployed fifth-generation stealth fighter in the world. This Raptor is assigned to the 49th Fighter Wing, Holloman AFB, New Mexico, and is backing away from a KC-135 Stratotanker. The Raptor today is conducting combat missions in the world's most frenetic and violent region, the Middle East. *USAF/Airman 1st Class J. Linzmeier*

The F-16 Falcons of the United States Air Force have undergone constant improvements and upgrades and are projected to remain in service until 2025, at which time they will be replaced by the Lockheed Martin F-35 Lightning II. The Israeli F-16A/B Netz and F-16C/D Barak have been augmented by the F-16I Sufa and are also projected to continue flying for the foreseeable future. The two photographs of F-16I No. 253 from Negev Squadron set against a stunning desert sunset demonstrate the numerous upgrades made to the F-16 Netz.

F-16I No. 253 from Negev Squadron taxiing prior to takeoff from Ramon Air Base. The Sufa is configured for a combat mission, armed with American made AIM-120 AAMs, along with two Rafael Python 5s. No. 253 is also armed with two GBU-15 glide bombs used to destroy high value targets. *O. Zidon Collection*

F-16I No. 253 clearly depicts the drastic changes made to the F-16I from the original F-16 Netz of the IASF. The F-16I now has the ability to carry a heavier load of offensive and defensive weapons. Communications, navigation, and targeting pods have all been upgraded, allowing the Sufa to engage in deeper penetration missions. The two photographs of No. 253 silhouetted against a brilliant desert sunset may have been taken during Operation CAST LEAD 2008. *O. Zidon Collection*

The Russian Bear and Chinese Dragon

Today, the United States and its allies are confronted almost daily with worldwide threats of military confrontation with the Russians in Eastern Europe and China and North Korea in the Pacific. The Israelis have no shortage of enemies in the Middle East. Looming largest for the Israeli Defense Forces at the moment is Iran, with its unrelenting threats to destroy Israel, and of course the United States.

In response to the messages of intimidation and defiance from Russian President Vladimir Putin, American F-15 Eagles have been forward deployed along with F-22 Raptors to Europe in support of NATO. The same events are playing out in the Pacific, where the Chinese have become an aggressor nation. The Russians and Chinese have spent billions of Rubles and Chinese Yuan on weapons systems to foster their political and military ambitions. Both countries have invested heavily in military aircraft. The Russians have produced the new Sukhoi T-50, an alleged fifth generation stealth fighter, while the Chinese are developing the J-31 Falcon Hawk and J-20 Mighty Dragon, both of which have become potential adversaries for US F-15s and F-22s.

The most recent documented fixed-wing aerial victory to date was claimed on 23 March 2014, when an F-16 from 182 Filo (Turkish Air Force) downed a Syrian Air Force MiG-23MB that intruded into Turkish airspace. This may not be the last in this part of the world, as evidence suggests Vladimir Putin may be ramping up Russian military involvement in Syria. Reports indicate the Russians have already deployed Sukhoi Su-30 Flanker-Cs to an airfield in Latakia, Syria.

The Russian deployment of tactical fighter aircraft in Syria will inevitably prove to be inherently dangerous. With the United States coalition actively engaged in air operations in Iraq and Syria against ISIS, the introduction of fourth generation Russian fighters like the Su-30SM Flanker, Su-24 Fencer, and Su-25 Frogfoot ground attack aircraft into the mix could bring coalition aircraft into an inadvertent confrontation with the Russians. The Su-30SM is a capable fourth generation fighter, but F-15s of the USAF and ISAF in the hands our elite pilots will prove to be more than adequate to deal with them.

The last time Russian pilots ventured into combat air operations in the Middle East was 30 July 1970, when five Russian pilots flying Egyptian MiG-21s were shot down in a well-orchestrated IAF ambush (Operation Rimon 20).

Aerial combat (dogfighting) may well be a thing of the past, but its complete demise may be premature. Technology in weapons and aircraft continue to advance, making beyond visual range (BVR) combat still quite relevant. The F-15s and F-16s of the USAF and IASF continue to evolve, training in air-to-air combat tactics for beyond visual range (BVR) and within visual range (WVR).

With the projected service lives of the F-15 Eagle and F-16 Falcon, it seems inevitable these iconic combat aircraft will add to their aerial combat victories in the future.

EPILOGUE

Many ask do the fourth generation F-15s and F-16s have what it takes to dominate the battle space in air-to-air combat in today's environment? American and Israeli aviation have long enjoyed nearly total air superiority during recent conflicts by deploying the most advanced operational warplanes, along with the best trained pilots in the world.

While in the service of the United States military (USAF, USN, and USMC) and the Israeli Defense Forces (IASF), the American-built F-15 Eagle and F-16 Falcon have time and time again proven that in the right hands these two combat tested aircraft have no equal.

With constant upgrades and modifications made to the Eagle and Falcon, they are more sophisticated and lethal than any time in their history. Boeing is producing a new configuration that allows the F-15SE to carry sixteen air-to-air missiles instead of the standard eight it now carries. The addition of conformal fuel tanks, extending the range of the Eagle and Falcon, and continued updates in electronics and sensors help increase their survivability in combat.

Like the aircraft of the Vietnam era, the weapon systems—such as the AIM-9X Sidewinder and AIM-7 Sparrow—have also evolved into newer and more lethal weapons. The Sidewinders and Sparrows have been joined by the new Raytheon AIM-120 AMRAAM. The AIM-120 all-aspect "fire-and-forget missile" has already proven highly effective in combat. The AIM-120—also known as the Slammer—is in the process of replacing the AIM-7 Sparrow. Israel has also introduced two new air-to-air weapon systems: the Rafael Python 5, with its electro-optical imaging seeker, may be the world's best air-to-air missile. The Rafael Derby, also known as the Alto, is another Israeli medium-range beyond visual range (BVR) active radar-homing missile.

So to the question. Do the Eagles and Falcons have what it takes to dominate today's modern battle space? The answer is a resounding yes—they can. However, the United States must continue to develop a new generation of aircraft beyond the F-22 Raptor and air-to-air weapons to maintain total air superiority in wars we are fighting today and are likely to encounter in the years ahead.

APPENDIX A

ISRAELI F-15 BAZ KILLS

DATE	TAIL NO.	AIRCREW	KILL WEAPON	KILL
27 June 1979	663	Moshe Melnik	Python 3	MiG-21
27 June 1979	704	Yoel Feldsho	AIM-7F	MiG-21
27 June 1979	672	Yoram Peled	AIM-9G	MiG-21
27 June 1979	689	Eitan-Ben Eliyahu	Cannon	MiG-21
24September 1979	695	Avner Naveh	AIM-7F	MiG-21
24 September 1979	695	Avner Naveh	AIM-9G	MiG-2166-0016
24 September 1979	676	Debi Rosenthal	AIM-7F	MiG-21
29 September 1979	692	Relik Shafir	AIM-9G	MiG-21
24 August 1980	696	Ilan Margalit	AIM-7F	MiG-21
31 December 1980	646	Yair Rachmilevic	AIM-9G	MiG-21
31 December 1980	695	Yoav Stern	Python 3	MiG-21 *
13 February 1981	672	Benny Zinker	AIM-7F	MiG-25
29 July 1981	673	Shaul Simon	AIM-7F	MiG-25
7 June 1982	658	Offer Lapidot	Python 3	MiG-23
8 June 1982	957	Schwartz/Reuven	AIM-7F	MiG-21
8 June 1981	686	Yoram Hoffman	AIM-7F	MiG-21
8 June 1982	818	Shaul Simon	AIM-7F	MiG-23 **
8 June 1982	832	Dedi Rosenthal	AIM-7F	MiG-23 ***
9 June 1982	684	Ronen Shapira	AIM-7F	MiG-23
9 June 1982	658	Gil Rapaport	AIM-7F	MiG-23
9 June 1982	802	Moshe Melnik	AIM-7F	MiG-23
9 June 1982	646	Avi Maor	Python 3	MiG-23
9 June 1982	802	Moshe Melnik	Python 3	MiG-21
9 June 1982	646	Avi Maor	Cannon	MiG-21
9 June 1982		Squadron Kill		MiG-23
9 June 1982		Squadron Kill		MiG-23
9 June 1982	684	Yoram Peled	Python 3	MiG-21

DATE	TAIL NO.	AIRCREW	KILL WEAPON	KILL
9 June 1982	686	Ronen Shapira	Python 3	MiG-21
9 June 1982	695	Oran Hampel	AIM-7F	MiG-21
10 June 1982	957	Naveh/Cohen	AIM-7F	MiG-23
10 June 1982	957	Naveh/Cohen	Python 3	MiG-23
10 June 1982	957	Naveh/Cohen	Python 3	MiG-21
10 June 1982	848	Ziv Nadivi	Python 3	Gazelle
10 June 1982	840	Benny Zinker	Python 3	MiG-23
10 June 1982	828	Gil Rapaport	Python 3	MiG-23
10 June 1982	802	Noam Knaani	Python 3	MiG-23
10 June 1982	802	Noam Knaani	Python 3	MiG-23
10 June 1982	708	Schwartz/Shapira	Python 3	MiG-21
10 June 1982	848	Yoram Hoffman	Cannon	MiG-21
10 June 1982	955	Mickey Lev	Python 3	MiG-21
10 June 1982	979	Peled/Zvi	Python 3	MiG-21
10 June 1982	667	Yiftach Shadmi	Python 3	MiG-21
11 June 1982	678	Yoram Peled	AIM-7F	MiG-23
11 June 1982	678	Yoram Peled	AIM-7F	MiG-23
11 June 1982	840	Yiftach Shadmi	AIM-7F	MiG-21
11 June 1982	704	Simon/Amir	AIM-7F	MiG-21
11 June 1982	646	Offer Lapidot	Python 3	MiG-21
24 June 1982	979	Feldsho/Zvi	Python 3	MiG-23
24 June 1982	979	Feldsho/Zvi	Python 3	MiG-23
31 August 1982	821	Shaul Schwartz	AIM-7F	MiG-25 ****
19 November 1985	840	Avner Naveh	Python 3	MiG-23
19 November 1985	840	Avner Naveh	Python 3	MiG-23 *****
19 November 1985	957	Ben-Dor/Paz	Python 3	MiG-23 ******

* Shared victory with F-4E aircrew

** Shared victory with Rosenthal

***Shared victory with Simon

****Shared victory with SAM Hawk battery

***** Shared victory with Ben-Dor and Paz

****** Shared victory with Naveh

APPENDIX B

ISRAELI F-16 NETZ KILLS

DATE	TAIL NO.	AIRCREW	KILL WEAPON	KILL
Knights of the North				
14 July 1981	219	Amir Nachumi	AIM-9L	MiG-21
9 June 1982	220	Amir Nachumi	AIM-9L	MiG-21
9 June 1982	223	Relik Shafir	AIM-9L	MiG-21
8 June 1982	225	Shlomo Sas	AIM-9L	MiG-23
11 June 1982	225	Relik Shafir	AIM-9L	Su-22
11 June 1982	225	Relik Shafir	AIM-9P3	Su-22
9 June 1982	232	Relik Shafir	AIM-9L	MiG-21
10 June 1982	234	Amir Nachumi	AIM-9L	MiG-23
10 June 1982	234	Amir Nachumi	AIM-9L	MiG-23
10 June 1982	234	Amir Nachumi	Maneuver	MiG-23
9 June 1982	237	Opher Einav	AIM-9L	MiG-21
10 June 1982	237	Amir Nachumi	AIM-9L	MiG-23
10 June 1982	237	Amir Nachumi	AIM-9L	MiG-23
25 May 1982	240	Amos Mohar	Unknown	MiG-21
25 May 1982	240	Amos Mohar	Unknown	MiG-21
11 June 1982	240	Yehuda Bavli	AIM-9L	Su-22
8 June 1982	242	Dubi Ofer	AIM-9L	MiG-23
9 June 1982	243	Avishai Canaan	AIM-9L	MiG-21
11 June 1982	246	Roee Tamir	AIM-9L	MiG-21
8 June 1982	250	Avishai Canaan	AIM-9L	MiG-21
9 June 1982	250	Roee Tamir	AIM-9L	MiG-21
9 June 1982	255	Avi Lavi	AIM-9L	MiG-21
7 August 2006	364	Classified	Python 4	UAV

DATE	TAIL NO.	AIRCREW	KILL WEAPON	KILL
"First Jet" Squadron				
21 April 1982	107	Zeev Raz	AIM-9L	MiG-23
9 June 1982	107	Eliezer Shkedi	AIM-9L	MiG-23
9 June 1982	107	Eliezer Shkedi	AIM-9L	MiG-23
11 June 1982	107	Eytan Stibbe	AIM-9L	Su-22
11 June 1982	107	Eytan Stibbe	Cannon	Su-22
11 June 1982	107	Eytan Stibbe	AIM-9L	MiG-23
11 June 1982	107	Eytan Stibbe	AIM-9P3	Gazelle
10 June 1982	111	Sasha Levin	AIM-9L	MiG-21
10 June 1982	111	Sasha Levin	AIM-9L	Gazelle
28 April 1981	112	Rafi Berkovich	Cannon	Mi-8
13 June 1985	112	Itzhak Gat	AIM-9L	DR-3
10 June 1982	116	Rafi Berkovich	AIM-9L	MiG-23
10 June 1982	116	Rafi Berkovich	AIM-9L	MiG-23
10 June 1982	116	Rafi Berkovich	Cannon	MiG-21
10 June 1982	118	Hagai Katz	AIM-9L	MiG-23
10 June 1982	124	Shlomo Zaytman	AIM-9L	MiG-23
28 April 1981	126	Dubi Yoffe	AIM-9	Mi-8
9 June 1982	129	Eytan Stibbe	AIM-9L	MiG-23
10 June 1982	138	Ami Lustig	Cannon	MiG-23
10 June 1982	252	Amos Bar	Cannon	Su-22
11 June 1982	254	Dani Oshrat	AIM-9L	MiG-21
11 June 1982	254	Dani Oshrat	AIM-9L	Su-22
11 June 1982	258	Rani Falk	AIM-9L	Su-22
11 June 1982	258	Rani Falk	Cannon	MiG-21
25 April 2013	340	Classified	Python 5	Ababil UAV
Ha Negve Squadron				
(?) June 1982	272	Moshe Rozenfeld	Unknown	MiG-21
21 April 1982	284	Hagai Katz	AIM-9L	MiG-23
First Squadron				
6 October 2012	844	Classified	Python 5	UAV

APPENDIX C
USAF F-15 Eagle Kills

DATE	TAIL NO.	AIRCREW	KILL WEAPON	KILL
17 January 1991	85-0125	Jon K. Kelk	AIM-7M	MiG-29
17 January 1991	85-0105	Rob Graeter	AIM-7M	Mirage F-1
17 January 1991	83-0017	Steve Tate	AIM-7M	Mirage F-1
17 January 1991	85-0108	Rhory Draeger	AIM-7M	MiG-29
17 January 1991	85-0107	Charles Magill	AIM-7M	MiG-29 *
19 January 1991	85-0099	Larry Pitts	AIM-7M	MiG-25
19 January 1991	85-0101	Richard Tollini	AIM-7M	MiG-25
19 January 1991	85-0122	CraigUnderhill	AIM-7M	MiG-29
19 January 1991	85-0114	Cesar Rodriguez	Maneuvering	MiG-29
19 January 1991	79-0021	David Sveden	AIM-7M	Mirage F-1
19 January 1991	79-0069	David Prather	AIM-7M	Mirage F-1
26 January 1991	85-0104	Anthony Schiavi	AIM-7M	Mirage F-1
26 January 1991	85-0114	Cesar Rodriguez	AIM-7M	MiG-23
27 January 1991	84-0027	Benjamin Powell	AIM-7M	Mirage F-1
27 January 1991	84-0027	Benjamin Powell	AIM-9M	MiG-23
27 January 1991	84-0025	Jay Denny	AIM-9M	MiG-23
27 January 1991	84-0025	Jay Denny	AIM-7M	MiG-23
28 January 1991	84-0022	Donald Watrous	AIM-7M	MiG-23
29 January 1991	84-0102	David Rose	AIM-7M	MiG-23

DATE	TAIL NO.	AIRCREW	KILL WEAPON	KILL
2 February 1991	79-0074	Gregory Masters	AIM-7M	Il-76
6 February 1991	84-0019	Robert Hehemann	AIM-7M	Su-25
6 February 1991	84-0019	Robert Hehemann	AIM-9M	Su-25
6 February 1991	79-0078	Thomas Dietz	AIM-9M	MiG-21
6 February 1991	79-0078	Thomas Dietz	AIM-9M	MiG-21
7 February 1991	85-0102	Anthony Murphy	AIM-7M	Su-20/22
7 February 1991	85-0102	Anthony Murphy	AIM-7M	Su-20/22
7 February 1991	85-0124	Rick Parsons	AIM-7M	Su-20/22
7 February 1991	80-0003	Randy May	AIM-7M	Mi-8
11 February 1991	79-0048	Steve Dingee	AIM-7M	Mi-8
11 February 1991	80-0012	Mark McKenzie	AIM-7M	Mi-8
14 February 1991	89-0487	Bennett/Bakke	GAU-8	Helo
20 February 1991	84-0014	John Doneski	AIM-9M	Su-22M
22 March 1991	84-0010	Thomas Dietz	AIM-9M	Su-22M
22 March 1991	84-0015	Robert Hehemann	Maneuver	PC-9
24 March 1999	86-0169	Cesar Rodriguez	AIM-120A	MiG-29
24 March 1999	86-0159	Mike Shower	AIM-120A	MiG-29
26 March 1999	86-0156	Jeff Hwang	AIM-120A	MiG-29

*Capt. Magill (USMC) on 17 January 1991 was a Marine Corps exchange pilot flying with the 58th TFS / 33rd TFW

Note: On 24 January 1991, Royal Saudi Air Force F-15 pilot Capt. Ayhed Salah al-Shamrani was credited with destroying 2 Iraqi Mirage F-1EQs whilst flying with the Coalition.

APPENDIX D

F-16 FALCON AERIAL COMBAT VICTORIES

DATE	TAIL NO.	AIRCREW	KILL WEAPON	KILL
Pakistani Air Force				
17 May 1986	82723	A. Hameed Qadri	AIM-9P	Su-22 (2)
30 March 1987	Unknown	Abdul Razzaq	AIM-9	AN-26
16 April 1987	85722	Badar-ul-Islam	AIM-9P	Su-22
4 August 1988	85725	Akhtar I. Bokhari	AIM-9P	Su-25
12 September 1988	85728	Khalid Mahmood	AIM-9	MiG-23 MLD (2)
3 November 1988	84717	Khalid Mahmood	AIM-9	Su-22
20 November 1988	Unknown	M. A. Khattak	AIM-9	AN-26
31 January 1989	85711	Khalid Mahmood	AIM-9	AN-24
7 June 2002	83605	Ayub/Aman	AIM-9L	UAV
Venezuelan Air Force				
27 November 1992	Unknown	Beltran Vielma	AIM-9P	OV-10
27 November 1992	Unknown	Helimenas Labarca	AIM-9P (?)	AT-27
United States Air Force				
27 December 1992	90-0778	Gary L. North	AIM-120	MiG-25
17 January 1993	86-0262	Craig D. Stevenson	AIM-120	MiG-23
28 February 1994	89-2137	Robert G. Wright	AIM-120	J-21
28 February 1994	89-2137	Robert G. Wright	AIM-9	J-21
28 February 1994	89-2137	Robert G. Wright	AIM-9	J-21
28 February 1994	89-2009	Steven L. Allen	AIM-120	J-21
April 1999	91-0353	Michael H. Geczy	AIM-120	MiG-29
Royal Netherlands Air Force				
24 March 1999	J-063	Peter Tankink	AIM-120	MiG-29
Turkish Air Force				
16 September 2013	92-0005	Classified	AIM-9	Hi-17
23 March 2014	91-0008	Classified	AIM-120	MiG-23MB
16 May 2015	Unknown	Classified	Unknown	Helicopter
16 October 2015	Unknown	Classified	AIM-9	Orlan 10Drone
24 November 2015	Unknown	Classified	Aim-120C7	Su-24M2